MW01706701

Feng Shui for Retailers

Written & Illustrated by
Linda Cahan

ST MEDIA GROUP INTERNATIONAL
Cincinnati, Ohio

ISBN 0-944094-05-8

Published by:

ST Books
ST Media Group International Inc.
407 Gilbert Avenue
Cincinnati, Ohio 45202 USA
Tel. 513-421-2050 • Fax 513-421-6110
E-mail: books@stmediagroup.com
www.stmediagroup.com/stbooks

For more information about the author:
www.lindacahan.com and/or www.visualseminars.com

Cover and book design by Benjamine Morrison

Design production by Jaxon Cook

Edited by Jenny Reising

Printed in the United States of America

9 8 7 6 5 4 3 2 1

Dedication

This book is dedicated to my dear friend, Jill Dotlo, who introduced me to Feng Shui.

With Deep Appreciation

To Mark Kissling, my fearless publisher and to Jenny Reising, my editor.

To Martin Pegler, who encouraged me to write this book – many times.

To Bill Cahan, my brother, for his generous support and love.

To my husband, Chris Stopa, whose love is my support.

To Wendye Pardue, an excellent Feng Shui practitioner, for editing the content of this book.

To Sandra Comas, who gave this book shape and clarity.

To all the supportive people in the Feng Shui community, whose help and advice was invaluable –

Stephen Devine

Elliot Jay Tanzer

Denise Linn

Terah Kathryn Collins

David Daniel Kennedy

Lillian Too

William Spear

INTRODUCTION

For You, the Reader

Any person in the retail field who has an interest in improving or fine-tuning his or her retail environment is the perfect reader of this text. A retailer with a full-line department store and a vendor with a cart can take the concepts from this book and apply them equally to their unique retail worlds. No matter what type of store you're affiliated with, your merchandise or style of selling, if you're in retail, this book will make sense for your situation.

If you are going to open a store, move into a new space, renovate or redecorate, read this book before you sign the lease or approve the architectural plans.

Do I have to read the entire book or can I skip around?
This book is written in sequence yet each chapter stands on its own, allowing you to skip around as you desire. However, each chapter does build on the one before so although you can pick a page here and there, you will derive the greatest benefit from reading the book sequentially. If a particular section doesn't apply to your situation, skim over it until you get to something that hits home.

Chapter One gives a very brief history of Feng Shui, explains "energy," discusses some other schools of Feng Shui and teaches you how to use *Black Sect Tantric Buddhist Feng Shui* in your store. This chapter is a "don't miss," as everything relates back to the Bagua, which will be explained in the must-read first chapter.

Chapter Two continues with the basics of Feng Shui. The concepts of the elements and Yin/Yang will influence all your decisions and actions when you start making changes in your store. Understanding the elements and Yin/Yang are vital for making sure the changes you apply will be positive rather than negative.

A quick note about positive and negative: These terms are used continuously throughout this book.

Positive means all good things including a sense of well-being, excellent health, financial success, good public relations and enjoyable interpersonal relations within the store and with the customers.

Negative means not so good at all! A negative experience includes poor business, unhappy customers and staff, lots of sick time and an overall feeling of discomfort, misery and unease.

Chapter Three is all about location. This chapter will give you insight regarding a location or space for your store as well as provide a new outlook on the site of your existing store. While you might initially skip this chapter because you're not planning to move in the near future, please read it at some point. It *will* provide you with excellent information about your existing space and bring you some important insights that might influence your direction for the future.

Taking a walk through your store

Chapter Four starts with the first impressions your store makes from the parking lot through the front entrance. The cliché – "you only have one chance to make a good first impression" – is based on the truth. Take the quiz at the end of the chapter. The results might surprise you.

Chapter Five continues the walk through your store with an eye on fixture placement, aisles, dead zones and the all-important poison arrows. These are created by energy flowing quickly down sharp angles. People can feel very uncomfortable when standing in the line of a poison arrow. Learn how they affect your business and how to cure the problems they cause.

Problems – another word often used throughout this book. People develop an interest in Feng Shui for many reasons. Some see it as a wonderful addition to their already fabulous lives, while others might view it as a way to help soften or solve some of the problems in their work or home existence. While problems are often called challenges in this politically correct world, a problem isn't necessarily a negative. Sometimes it's an opportunity to rethink a way of presentation or a method of doing business. If the word "problem" becomes problematic for you, please substitute any of the following words: quandary, puzzle, dilemma, predicament, difficulty or setback.

Chapter Six could go almost anywhere in the book, but I chose to place it here. It's all about color. Color is such an important aspect of store design, image and presentation that the topic could have its own book. There is a lot of confusion and concern about the use of color combined with Feng Shui. This chapter will clear up the confusion and give you understandable ideas of how to use colors successfully in your store.

Chapter Seven continues our tour through the store with a discussion of the walls. They not only hold up the store, but they also tend to create the most visible impressions. This chapter discusses the elements, textures, fixtures, lights and merchandising of your walls. Please feel free to skip this chapter if you don't have walls. Otherwise, take the quick quiz at the end of the chapter to get a start on working with your walls to achieve greater balance, energy and sales.

Balance is another oft-used term. While balance traditionally means a harmonious arrangement, an equal distribution of weight and a state of equilibrium, in Feng Shui it most often refers to the elements and the Yin/Yang in your store. This important information is found in Chapter Two. Balance is often used to describe energy, lights, fixture placement, light and dark merchandise, and signs. Understanding Yin/Yang and the elements will aid in all your future plans for your store.

Chapter Eight discusses the spaces that can silently make or break your store. Retailers are understandably most concerned with what the customer sees rather than the back office, stockrooms, hallways, attic, basement and restrooms. Yet in Feng Shui, the entire leased or owned space is uniformly important and must be worked with equally. If you were looking forward to skipping this chapter, you will be missing important information that can lead to improving your store's overall energy and environment.

Chapter Nine is all about clearing your space, and the remedies or cures for the problems that keep your store from being as successful as you desire. While you might be tempted to check out this chapter first, please don't implement any of the cures or remedies until you've read the entire book. A little knowledge is a dangerous thing.

Chapter Ten is a quick, interesting read as it goes over the most commonly asked questions regarding Feng Shui and your store. It relates back to all the chapters in the book and acts as a reminder of some of what you've learned from Modern Feng Shui for Retailers.

Feng Shui for Retailers is the first book to be published on Feng Shui strictly for retailers. The retail information in this book has been accumulated over time by the author, but she has gratefully learned much about Feng Shui from many masters and their books and lectures.

References and Referrals is the section where all the Feng Shui experts quoted or referenced in this book are introduced to you with their listed books and contact information. Throughout this book, I am honored to use information I learned from the Feng Shui masters and teachers listed in References and Referrals. The people listed in this section are Feng Shui masters whose expertise will help you maximize your sales.

Examples will be used throughout this book whenever relevant. Some chapters have more, some far less. Please send me your examples. I would love to hear from you and share some of your stories with other readers. (info@lindacahan.com)

Quizzes are at the end of some chapters. They provide you with insight as well as a good opportunity to analyze and improve the Feng Shui in your store. Consider making extra copies before you fill in the page with your answers. These quizzes provide the best insights and analyses when you have several opinions.

If it ain't broke, don't fix it!

A store that is doing well with happy customers, sales staff and management has already followed, possibly intuitively, the principals of Feng Shui. When all is going well, using intelligent and instinctive retail know-how will often keep things moving smoothly. Major Feng Shui cures are best implemented when you move into a new space or renovate your existing space. Important Feng Shui changes can help stores that seem invisible or unlucky. Simpler cures work well when sales are slow (and not just because of the time of year) or when the store needs fine-tuning. Every space can stand some enhancement.

Don't worry and don't obsess. There is no perfection.

There is no such thing as a perfectly "Feng Shui-ed" store, home or business. Very often in order to fix or remedy one problem, you'll create or have to deal with another, lesser problem. All you can do is learn as much as you can and try to make intelligent changes based on your new knowledge and your existing retail experience. Start with the intention to enhance your life and the lives of the people around you through improving your business. Over time, you will be progressively in tune with things that are not in harmony with your intention. It's that simple.

It takes time, intention and action:

- Time to develop your instincts
- Intention to clearly know what you want
- Action to make the changes necessary to achieve your desires

TABLE OF CONTENTS

I

Getting Started

Retail is all about what's new, hot and different. It's all about people, moving in and out of a store and, most of all, it's about sales. Retailers are always trying to come up with ideas to create higher profits with less cash outlay. Sometimes the fixed expenses combined with emergencies leave little room for improvements. Consequently, many retailers look for solutions that aren't necessarily "MBA approved." The growing interest in Feng Shui throughout Western cultures is born from a strong need and desire to create happier, healthier and more successful retail environments in a new, more holistic and intuitive fashion.

A Very Short History of Feng Shui

Feng Shui is a study that has been in practice for more than 4,000 years. The words "Feng" and "Shui" mean "wind" and "water" in Chinese. The practice of Feng Shui started out as a way for families to honor their ancestors, thereby ensuring good luck, health and prosperity for their family's future. Honoring one's ancestors included making sure their burial plots were well situated to avoid storms and flooding. If the plots were located on the top of a hill, they would be battered by wind and rain. If at the bottom of a hill, they could easily flood. The ideal placement for a grave was halfway between the top and the bottom of the hill, allowing fresh water to flow freely past the grave without flooding the site. The hill protected the grave from extreme weather conditions. Over the years, the spiritual, intuitive and practical placement of burial sites grew to encompass the study of the best sites for homes and commerce. In ancient times, the ideal home was positioned with hills behind, water flowing swiftly past, and good, fertile soil.

That was 4,000 years ago, give or take a few hundred years. What began as a vital relationship between nature and mankind evolved into modern Feng Shui. When you lease or buy a retail space today, other stores and buildings often surround it. One rarely has full control over the exterior environment and, therefore, must place hope, faith and energy on the interior space. Learning about solutions to site placement problems in rural China thousands of years ago might not seem relevant to your retail issues at the local mall. For example, you will hopefully not have to worry about burial sites. However, the ancient concepts of Feng Shui have evolved through the centuries to embrace change, address new concerns and encompass our modern stores, current issues and lack of suitable choices in our locations.

The Basic Concepts of Feng Shui

"Feng Shui is the study of how to arrange your outer world to enhance your inner world."[☯] Some people might believe that Feng Shui is just a way to arrange furniture and objects in a space and, while that is a part of the practice, it is also the connection between our inner and outer lives. If you arrange your store to the best of your ability or budget but don't feel comfortable with the results, that "make-do" attitude will be reflected in your store and your underlying attitude. We can arrange our homes and stores to perfection but if our inner attitude is one of failure, we doom ourselves to repeat that attitude on the outside. One aspect of Feng Shui is to find ways to allow the energy in our stores to work for us to create success. Negativity can be combated both internally and externally. When you learn about Feng Shui, you take a big step toward strengthening your life in a positive manner.

Your intent to make the environment of your store more conducive to success is the first step in using Feng Shui to improve your environment.

Energy! You'll see a lot of this word. While I might refer to it as Chi or Qui just to mix it up, the English term "energy" is what you'll see most often. Energy has many meanings. The simple scientific explanation of energy is the capacity of something to do work. In this book, energy is referred to as the force that resides in all things, alive or manmade. The energy in natural things such as animals, minerals, plants, insects and humans requires a good flow in order to work. A lack of flow means it's stopped up in some way, such as a broken leg or stem, an excess of fat or

---

☯ *The Western Guide to Feng Shui Room* by Room by Terah Kathryn Collins www.hayhouse.com publisher and year?

cholesterol, or possibly it's inhibited from growth or movement by being stuck in a very low cave, under a rock or short ceiling. Manmade objects contain the energy of molecules but not the energy of life. They can create obstacles to the growth and movement of natural things. Manmade objects can also "hold" the energy of natural things through long-term use. This might sound a little strange, but the molecules in manmade things such as cash registers or wrap desks are influenced by the ever-moving natural energy that surrounds and permeates them.

Chi or Qui

Perhaps you've heard the term "chi" pronounced "chee." It means energy and is the unifying force of nature. People have chi, rocks have chi, even sheetrock has chi – but it's pretty hidden from view. Essentially all things have some sort of energy that runs through them and this energy is what makes up our environments and our lives. When we become aware of the energy, or chi, in both natural and manmade things, we can begin to find ways to allow that to work for us in positive and productive ways.

Energy needs to flow freely throughout a store because when trapped, it creates stagnant, dull areas. Arranging your store so that the energy flows smoothly and unobstructed will make the space more pleasurable for you, your staff and your customers. Trapped energy feels uncomfortable and lifeless. Salespeople tend to work less and with less enthusiasm in a store with trapped energy, while customers stay in the store for shorter times. Trapped energy occurs in dead-end aisles, clutter, dark spaces, unlit nooks and crannies, disorganized stockrooms, restrooms, crowded hallways and messy entrances. It can also occur at the checkout counter, in the office or on the loading dock. Trapped energy can slow down sales.

More than 4,000 years ago, Feng Shui was fairly simple, but over time it has accumulated many layers and theories. It is now considered to be complicated with many viewpoints and methods of practice. If you look in your local bookstore, you will find anywhere from five to 55 different books explaining Feng Shui. This book will simplify and make clear a method of Feng Shui that will work well for your store. What you learn from reading this book will start you on your path to improving the good fortune in your life.

Schools of Feng Shui

The job of a consultant is to solve past and current problems and foresee and prevent future problems. In order to set him or herself apart, a Feng Shui consultant or master looked at a problem and tried to solve it in a new way. Imagine more than 4,000 years of consultants and masters finding new and more intricate ways of analyzing, preventing and solving problems, and you understand why there are many excellent schools of Feng Shui – and so much confusion. One can read a book by one master that will contradict another. One school of Feng Shui sees your money section in the southwest section of your store while another sees it in the far left ninth corner of your store. In order to understand and implement Feng Shui, it makes sense to work with one philosophy.

This book focuses on the Black Sect Tantric Buddhist Feng Shui School and relates it to retail stores. This school of Feng Shui is very popular in Western Europe and The United States. It is the ideal form of Feng Shui for retailers because it works from the front door as opposed to the traditional directional Compass School that aligns with North, South, East and West. Aligning from the front door is how customers enter your space and "read" your store. This will be explained thoroughly as you read this chapter.

Other important schools are Flying Star Feng Shui, Eight Mansion Feng Shui, Form School and Compass Feng Shui. They are each fascinating and powerful. As they rely on astrological information, numerology and compass directions, they can be difficult to learn and apply to a retail store. If you want to delve deeper into these different methods after reading this book, you will find resources and different types of practitioners and masters listed in the Referrals section.

The cures, suggestions and changes discussed in this book will work for most retail problems. Sometimes things get more complicated and you need the help of a master Feng Shui practitioner.

If, after you apply Feng Shui changes in your store you are still experiencing serious problems, find a master in Flying Star or Compass Feng Shui. The master will work with the astrological aspects of the owner and the "birth" of the store. The changes he or she will suggest might be radical but if you are experiencing radical problems, it is worth making the changes. There is a list in the back of the book with the contact information for Feng Shui schools and some masters from around the United States.

Black Sect Tantric Buddhist Feng Shui

This highly spiritual school of Feng Shui was developed by Master Lin Yun as a fusion of classic Chinese beliefs and shamanic traditions from Tibet. He was trained from childhood by Tibetan monks in the practice of Feng Shui and has translated this ancient practice into Western culture. While

BSTBFS or "Black Sect" is not only highly metaphysical and intuitive in its origins, it is also the most understandable and practical form of Feng Shui for retailers. Its base is traditional Chinese Feng Shui – the understanding of the impact of energy and elements on people, their health, happiness, success in their homes and businesses.

The "Black Sect" tradition includes prayer and manifesting intentions. Rather than using a directional compass, the Bagua map works from the front door of the store – also known as "the compass of the heart."

The Bagua

The Bagua map is based on the *I Ching*, the Book of Changes. Each of the eight sections of the Bagua is called a trigram, and each of these trigrams is associated with a blessing of life. The blessings include friends and family, wealth, health, helpful people, creativity and children, wisdom and knowledge, fame, career and loving relationships. The Bagua map is used to enhance each of these areas in your store.

Your intention to make positive changes, combined with the placement of meaningful objects in the correct places, will bring about new energies and luck in your store.

How to Work with the Bagua

To use this map, imagine that the front door of your store lies in the entrance area. The door will either be in Knowledge, Career or Helpful Friends. Now imagine your store as if it's a floor plan. Lay an imaginary grid over the store, dividing it into nine equal squares. Your store might not be a square or rectangle – you might have an odd shape or have areas missing from the Bagua map. Don't worry! This is normal and there are solutions to almost every problem.

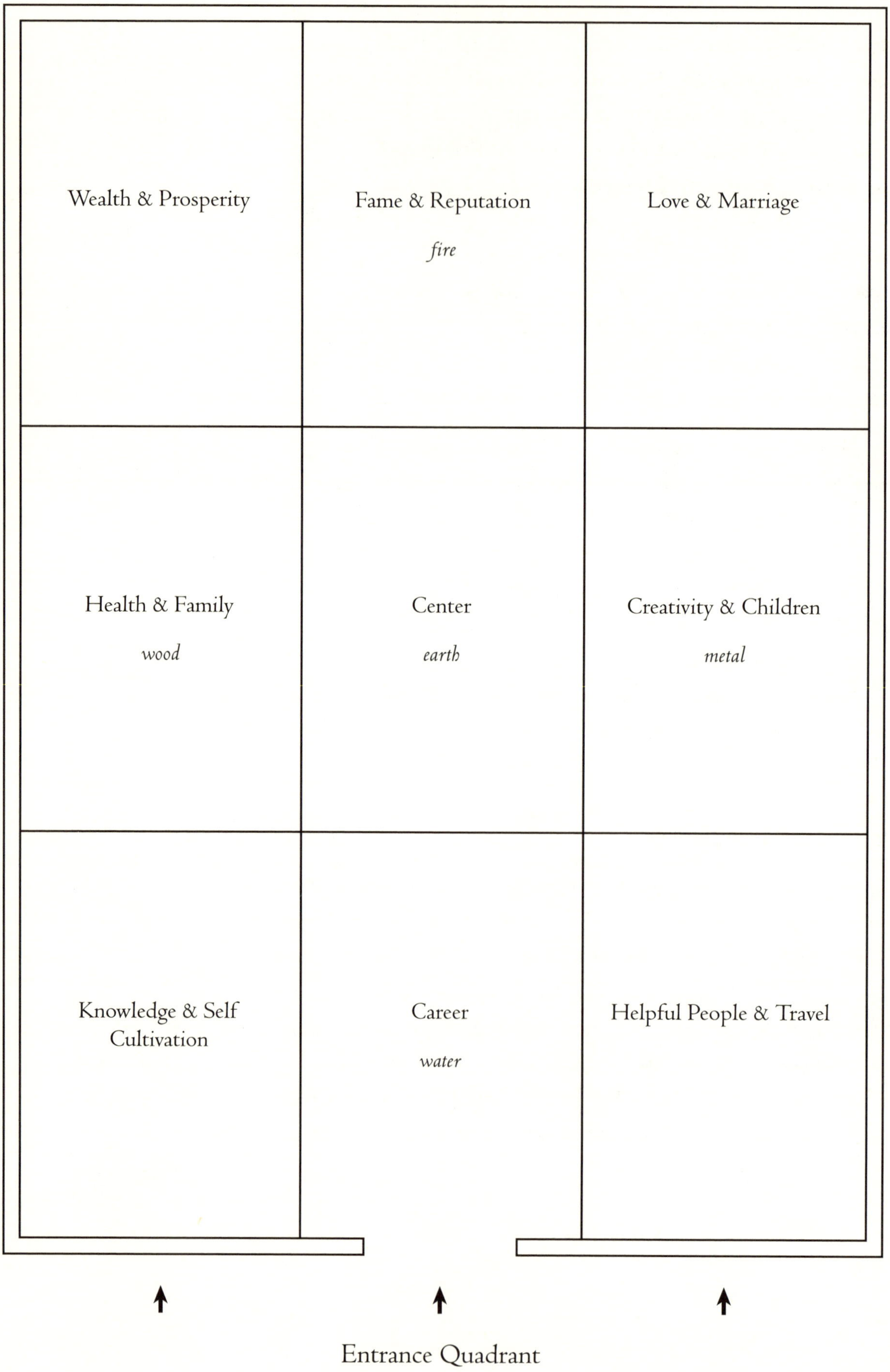
Wealth & Prosperity
Fame & Reputation
fire
Love & Marriage
Health & Family
wood
Center
earth
Creativity & Children
metal
Knowledge & Self Cultivation
Career
water
Helpful People & Travel
Entrance Quadrant

Make it simple for yourself. Sketch out your store on an 8½-by-11-inch sheet of paper. Don't worry about fixtures; just sketch the outline of the exterior walls of the entire leased space. Inside this space plan add your office, stockroom and toilet areas (including doors), and your front and back doors. For those among you who are detail oriented and somewhat compulsive, pull out your ruler and draw two equally spaced lines through your store – top to bottom and left to right, creating a grid with nine equal spaces. For you spontaneous types, eyeball it and draw your lines. Note whether your door lies in the Knowledge, Career or Helpful People/Travel area.

The rest of your store will lay out easily from this point. Your Wealth section is always in the far left ninth corner of your store. Relationships are always in the far right ninth area.

If your store has more than one level, the map applies to each floor in the same way. On the second floor, the wealth section will be above the one on the first floor. The Bagua map is the same for every floor of your store. Its layout is always determined from the location of the front door.

The Bagua map works for individual departments or rooms as well. If you just want to do a Feng Shui enhancement to your office, sketch it out and lay the grid over it, seeing your office door in the Knowledge, Career or Helpful People/Travel sections.

Your stockroom, office and washrooms are included in the map. The map is for your entire leased space – not just the selling floor.

Missing Areas in Your Store

Not all stores are rectangular or square. Very often you share a wall or two with other tenants and your space might be

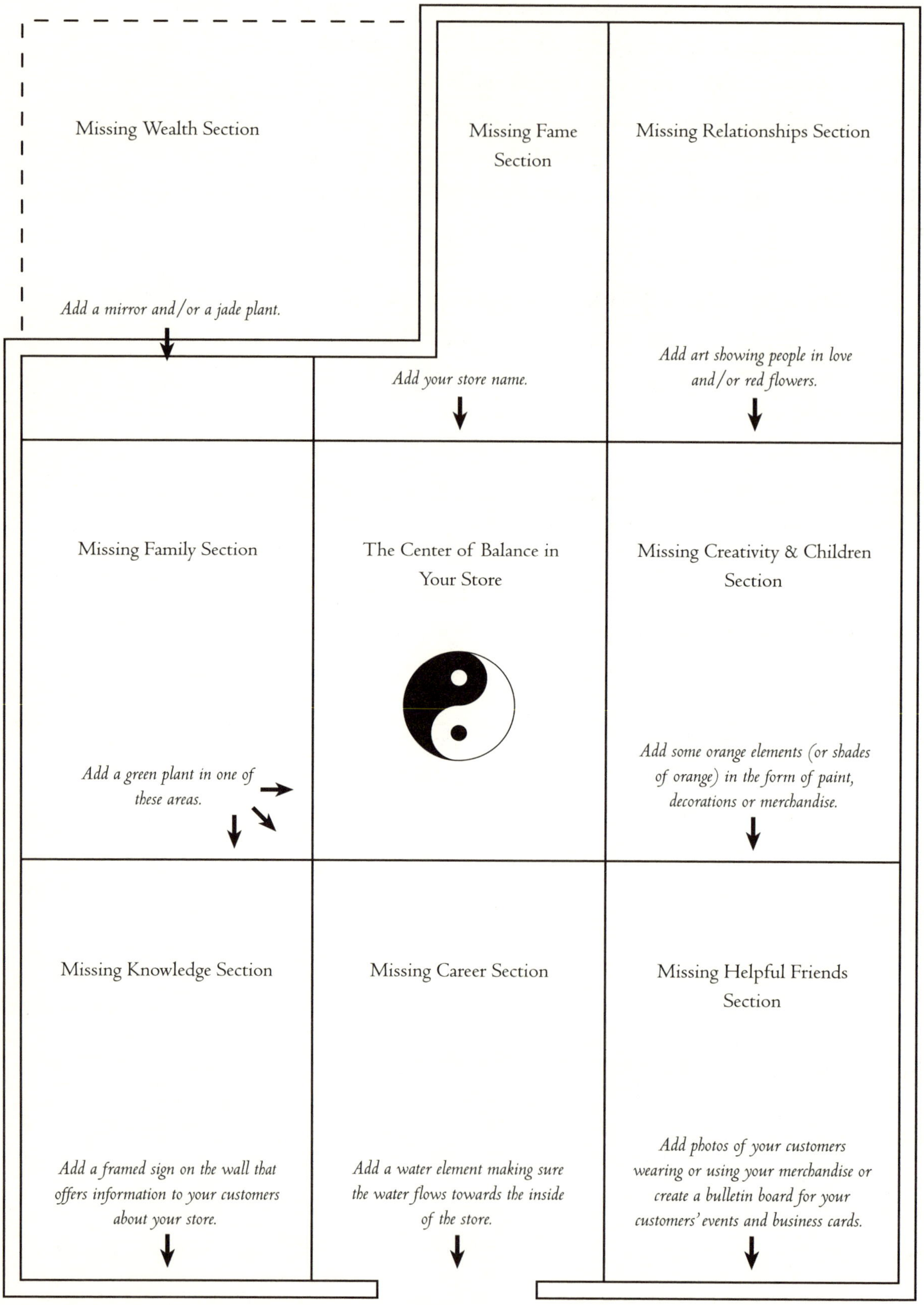
Missing Wealth Section
Add a mirror and/or a jade plant.
Missing Fame Section
Add your store name.
Missing Relationships Section
Add art showing people in love and/or red flowers.
Missing Family Section
Add a green plant in one of these areas.
The Center of Balance in Your Store
Missing Creativity & Children Section
Add some orange elements (or shades of orange) in the form of paint, decorations or merchandise.
Missing Knowledge Section
Add a framed sign on the wall that offers information to your customers about your store.
Missing Career Section
Add a water element making sure the water flows towards the inside of the store.
Missing Helpful Friends Section
Add photos of your customers wearing or using your merchandise or create a bulletin board for your customers' events and business cards.

missing a Bagua area. An area is considered missing when it is a full one-ninth of your store.

If this is the case, you want to pretend this area exists by adding symbolic elements to enhance the existing area and suggest the missing one. For example, if your wealth section is missing, you will want to put a mirror on the wall where the area would start. It is best if this mirror is not visible from the front door. You never want to reflect cars (energy moving away from your store), staircases (energy moving up or down) or bathrooms (energy/money being flushed down the toilet). If the mirror used to symbolically "fill in" a missing section of the Bagua is visible from the front door, place a higher fixture in front of it so the merchandise is doubled by the reflection. A mirror strengthens the existing area by keeping the energy inside the store.

Symbolic Elements for Missing Sections

Missing Wealth: Add a jade plant in the far left corner of your store to symbolize wealth.
Missing Relationships: Add a picture of two people dancing, walking or interacting romantically. Red flowers or flowering plants in this area will work as well.
Missing Fame: Add your store name – big!
Missing Knowledge: Add a framed sign on the wall that offers information to your customers about your store, its history and purpose – keep it short and sweet.
Missing Helpful Friends: On a framed bulletin board, add pictures of your customers or letters from your customers praising your store. Hopefully you've received a few in the course of doing business.
Missing Creativity/Children: Add some orange elements either through paint or decorative items.
Missing Family: Add a green plant in this area.

Enhancing the Bagua Blessings Areas of Your Store

Remember the importance of your intention. Read the beginning of Chapter Ten before you implement a remedy for a missing area.

Intention: This term refers to your resolve, aim or purpose. An intention requires thought and an understanding that each action has a result and impact. Making an intention a reality means manifesting, or taking action and understanding the consequences of the action.

Think about what you want to manifest in your store before you apply the following enhancements. Some of these enhancements might seem strange or superstitious and others might not work with your store's image or décor. Pick what works for you or invent something that works with the identical feeling and intention. If one of your customers or friends is a Feng Shui practitioner, discuss your intention with her first before you implement an enhancement. These enhancements can be very powerful and require thought before you "throw one in a corner." As you learn, it is always good to get an educated opinion.

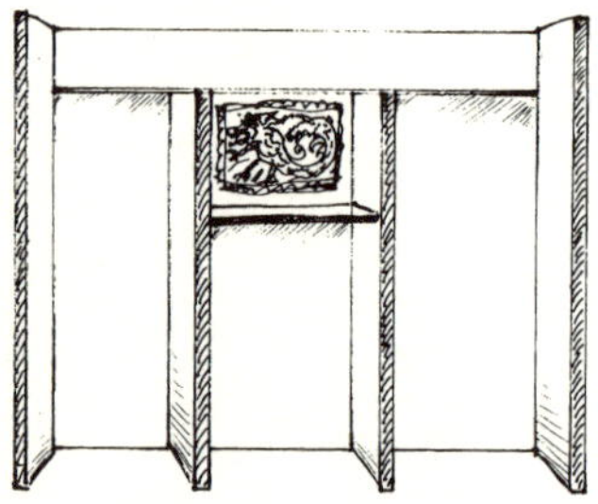

Wall breaks enhance the Friends and Family area as well as creating excellent merchandising opportunities for color or style stories.

Friends and Family – Your connection to your past, your ancestors and your ability to create a fruitful future can be enhanced by fruit symbols or fruit images. Other symbols include:

- Tall plants
- A dragon sculpture or painting
- Columns or wood wall breaks
- Stripes on the walls or merchandise

Wealth – This area represents the abundance, prosperity and appreciation of your life. Add a growing, healthy, green, round-leaved plant. Jade is ideal. Bamboo is also good. Other symbols include:

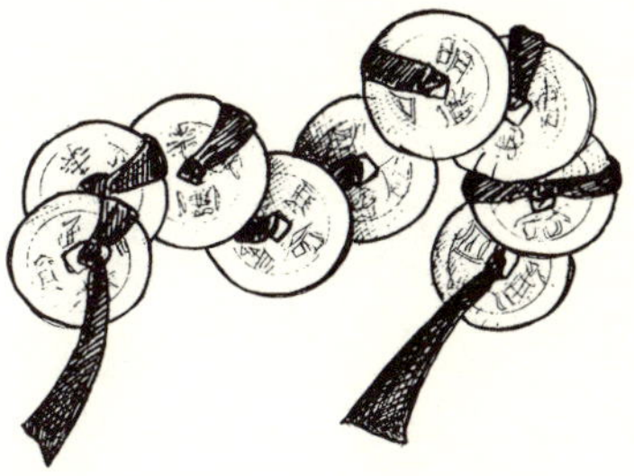

Nine Chinese coins tied with a red cord = Good Fortune.

- Chimes – of good quality with a pleasing sound. Cheap chimes = cheap results.
- Nine Chinese coins tied together with a red ribbon or cord
- Vertical wood elements such as wall breaks, columns or wood fixtures
- Moving objects – fans, either ceiling-mounted or upright
- A painting of a sailing ship with full sails and filled with treasure. The treasure part can be imagined or an actual part of the painting.
- A "three-legged" toad – in semiprecious stones, brass or copper. Avoid ones made of wood, pewter or silver. Gold tones are best. Place it diagonally to your front door approximately 2.5 to 3 feet from the floor on a table or fixture. According to Lillian Too, to attract wealth, avoid toads with Chinese symbols on their backs.
- Fill a "wealth vase" with three Chinese coins tied together with red thread or ribbon and semiprecious stones. The vase should be glass or ceramic with a large opening, a narrow neck and a wide base. Hide the vase in a cabinet – it's not for public view!
- The colors purple, red, silver or green

Wealth vase filled with coins and symbols of money and financial success.

Health – This is the center section of your store, the balance of Yin and Yang, light and dark, and health and illness. This is also the earth area of your store and is an excellent place for anything yellow or earth-toned. Consider putting live bamboo in a golden-yellow clay, glass or ceramic vase in the center of a table. (Yes, there can also be merchandise on the table – just place the vase higher and centered.) This area needs great lights to add balance to the rest of the store.

Other symbols of good fortune:

- The celestial dragon holding a pearl is the most powerful symbol of good fortune and wealth.
- The dragon tortoise with a baby tortoise on its back brings luck and wealth.
- The dragon horse can bring fame, wealth, honor and success.
- The dragon phoenix vase symbolizes happiness in marriage.

Helpful People, Networking and Travel – This section relates to attraction of new people, customers, employees, mentors and helpful people into your store and your life. It also relates to the release of negative people, products, employees and systems that don't work to your benefit or that of your store. Other symbols include:

• Metal lamps or picture frames of special people in your life or in the life of your store

Example: The successful chain of Jean Louis David hair salons in New York was named after its Parisian founder. There was always a photograph of Jean Louis David in each salon near the reception desk. Although Regis Corporation purchased the salons, the company chose to keep the original name and honor the founder by hanging his photo in a prominent position, often near the front door.

- Filing cabinets (if they make sense in your store design)
- Mementos from great travels
- Pictures of places and people that inspire you
- Any representation of spiritual guides and angels
- A trash can for sorting out the old and making room for the new (if it's under your checkout counter and not in public view)

Creativity and Children – How do you accept abundance in your life? This area represents your ability to enjoy prosperity as well as enhance your creativity. Gemstones and geodes are excellent in this area. Other symbols include:

- Rainbows and rainbow colors
- Anything round or circular – other than empty pots
- Open vases (put in some gold painted rocks to suggest money)
- A photograph or painting of a crane (bird)
- Metal bells or wind chimes

Knowledge and Wisdom– This area represents your expertise, cultivation and ability to communicate your wisdom to others. Books, magazines and educational brochures are ideal for this area. Other symbols include:

- Statues of Buddha
- Pottery or clay vases, rectangles or squares
- Large, heavy objects – rocks, huge vases
- A picture of the storeowner along with his/her personal philosophy for the store

Fame – This back sector is often the first wall that is seen when customers enter your store and is considered to be an important focal point. This area signals your reputation and image as well as how your store is perceived by others in the community. This is a good area for your store name, but a terrible area for a stockroom door! Other symbols include:

- Extra lighting or a great lamp
- Peony bush or painting of peonies or lotus blossoms
- A sculpture of a horse or phoenix
- Red or orange tones
- A triangular-shaped wall sculpture pointing up

Bring attention to your stores name by framing in with a frame that works with the style and image of your store.

A tortoise sculpture or a live turtle enhances the Career area.

Career – You might be welcoming customers in through this section of your store. The Career area is related not just to what you (as the storeowner) want to do in your life in terms of business or career. It is vital that this area is very clear about the store's intention and image as well. If you think you would prefer to be a writer, enhance that in your home, not in the store. The career section is an area of clarity and purpose for the customer. It must be about your current career in retail and not about other possibilities for your future. This is an excellent area for a water element such as a fountain (with the water flowing into the store – preferably toward the cash register). Other symbols include:

- Flowing tablecloth over a round table
- Organic-shaped vases with cascading silk or live flowers and leaves
- A tortoise sculpture or, if you're a nurturer by nature, a live tortoise in a safe, clean and beautiful environment. They can really smell if not cleaned regularly!
- Your mission statement on a sign in a decorative, image-appropriate sign holder

Two vases with two flowers represent loving and positive relationships.

Relationships – Long-lasting relationships are the cornerstones of retail success. Positive relationships between you and your customers, vendors, staff and community are vital to the long-lasting success of your store. Two of almost any object you deeply value can represent Intimate Relationships. Other symbols:

- Painting of two ducks, two people in love or two pink flowers
- Earthenware bowls – preferably rectangular or square
- Square or rectangular pillows in pink, taupe, beige and off-white

Some Helpful Hints from Terah Kathryn Collins

These ideas come from Terah Kathryn Collins, founder of Essential Feng Shui and The Western School of Feng Shui. They are taken from her article for *New Age Retailer* magazine.

Don't be concerned about interior walls. Depending on your store's layout, grid areas can span part of one large room or several small areas. (Grid in this article refers to the sections of the Bagua.)

When your front entrance is built on a diagonal, you'll have to make a judgment call as to which way to place the Grid. Often, it's the direction you look at first when you open the door.

When your front door is recessed, you might be entering your store through the Friends and Family, Center of Balance, or Children and Creativity Grid areas. If your front door is recessed all the way back, so that you immediately have to turn to enter the main part of the store, rotate the Grid to fit over the main body of the building.

You might find that one or more Grid areas correlate with what's working – or not working – in your business. For instance, many storeowners discover that a chaotic back room correlates with the Wealth and Prosperity area of the Grid, accurately reflecting their business's financial status. Prosperity begins to flow into their lives when they dig the room out and get organized.

As a storeowner, the Love and Marriage Grid area relates to partners, co-owners, key employees or other professionally "intimate" relationships you have as a result of being in business. The Friends and Family area relates to most employees, and the Helpful People and Travel section is associated with vendors, wholesalers and other helpful people who are located outside the store. Both the Children and

Creativity and Helpful People and Travel areas are directly related to customers. If any of these business relationships are not going well, work to improve the area that correlates with them.

REVIEW

Chapter One: Getting Started

1. Feng Shui is an ancient practice from China. It started with families honoring their ancestors with appropriate burial plots. The placement of plots evolved slowly over time to encompass homes and businesses.

2. "The art of placement" is a term often used to describe Feng Shui, yet the practice is far more complicated than moving objects artfully. Feng Shui also refers to the direct connection between your inner desires and your exterior surroundings. It is the relationship between the inside and outside of your being.

3. Intention describes not only what you want but also how you will take action to achieve your goals.

4. All things have some sort of energy that runs through them, and this energy is what makes up our environments and lives. The energy in natural things such as animals, minerals, plants, insects and humans requires a good flow in order to work. A lack of flow means it's stopped up in some way, and illness and blocked or bad luck may result from this blockage.

5. Black Sect Tantric Buddhist Feng Shui School. This school of Feng Shui is very popular in Western Europe and the

United States. It is the ideal form of Feng Shui for retailers because it works from the front door. Aligning from the front door is how customers enter your space and "read" your store. It is also a highly spiritual study where intention and all the thoughts and feelings behind actions determine the results.

6. The Bagua Map is used exclusively by the Black Sect School. All energy flows through one of three sections on the map – Knowledge, Career, or Helpful People and Travel. Every store, home or office can be partitioned in ninths using the Bagua map. Once a space is divided equally, each area is then addressed by its spiritual meaning combined with the intention of the storeowner or manager.

7. There are symbolic elements and objects for each area. If an area of your store needs strengthening, adding one of these elements is a start. It is vital that the addition of an element is done with an understanding of the intention behind the action along with consciousness.

8. Once you have laid out your store using the Bagua map and you discover that you have a missing section, there are remedies that can be applied to alleviate this problem. Mirrors are one of the most powerful cures. Be aware that whatever the mirror reflects is doubled. Do not double traffic rushing by stairwells, toilets, columns or anything that takes away energy from your selling floor.

QUIZ

Assess your Bagua grid by looking at each area of your store and determine:

1. What do I like/dislike about each space?

Friends and Family:

Wealth:

Center:

Helpful People:

Creativity/Children:

Wisdom/Knowledge:

Fame:

Career:

Relationships/Love:

2. What do I like/dislike about the things located in each area?

Friends and Family:

Wealth:

Center:

Helpful People:

Creativity/Children:

Wisdom/Knowledge:

Fame:

Career:

Relationships/Love:

3. What is my first thought when I see each area?

Friends and Family:

Wealth:

Center:

Helpful People:

Creativity/Children:

Wisdom/Knowledge:

Fame:

Career:

Relationships/Love:

4. Do I feel comfortable and safe, and would my customers feel comfortable and safe in each area?

Friends and Family:

Wealth:

Center:

Helpful People:

Creativity/Children:

Wisdom/Knowledge:

Fame:

Career:

Relationships/Love:

5. Is each part of the grid organized?

Friends and Family:

Wealth:

Center:

Helpful People:

Creativity/Children:

Wisdom/Knowledge:

Fame:

Career:

Relationships/Love:

6. What specific improvements or enhancements can I make?

Friends and Family:

Wealth:

Center:

Helpful People:

Creativity/Children:

Wisdom/Knowledge:

Fame:

Career:

Relationships/Love:

With much thanks to:

New Age Retailer, Terah Kathryn Collins, founder of Essential Feng Shui and The Western School of Feng Shui

The Illustrated Encyclopedia of Feng Shui by Lillian Too, 2000, Barnes & Noble Books

2

The Balance of the Elements and Yin and Yang

The Five Elements

As human beings, we are made up of all the basic elements in nature: water, earth, metal, wood and fire. Our bodies are composed of 90 percent water, and there are many different metals in our systems that are part of our blood and organs. Earth energy is represented by our connection to this planet, which includes the ever-present and always necessary gravity. Fire is our inner electrical system, our organs and blood.

For a human being to feel comfortable in a retail environment, the basic elements that are in nature and our bodies must be represented in the store and be in balance with each other. When an environment doesn't "feel" right, the first solution is to look at the balance of Yin, Yang and the elements in the space. At the end of the Elements section, you will find a Store Elements Analysis form to help you determine the balance in your store.

The Five Elements and a Vanilla Box Store

In a mall or strip center, a retailer might receive a "vanilla box" when leasing a store space. A vanilla box is comprised of sheetrock walls, fuzz on the floor, a suspended ceiling with fluorescent lights, a stockroom and a bathroom. The front door is very often glass and metal. The balance of natural elements in this space is minimal. Although all the elements are there, they are in a fairly unnatural form. Humans respond better to the elements being represented in as close to a natural state as possible.

The five elements are water, wood, fire, earth and metal. Below is a comparison of elements in a standard vanilla-box store and in the ideally balanced store.

Water may be represented literally by a water fountain or symbolically by flowing fabric.

Water

Vanilla box – Mirrors, glass and black or dark colors
Your store – Mirrors, crystals and glass, free-flowing shapes, real water features such as fountains or fish tanks, art depicting water, asymmetrical displays and arrangements, and black and dark colors as accents

Silk flowers not only represent the wood element but are an excellent display tool. Dried flowers are dead energy while good quality silks "live" forever.

Wood

Vanilla box – Columns and beams, wood floor (if you're lucky)
Your store – Wood fixtures, wood floors (when appropriate to your image), wood accessories, plants and potted flowers including silks, paper, art portraying gardens, plants, flowers and trees in a landscape, rounded columns, beams, the colors blue and green, and vertical stripes

Fire

Vanilla box – Fluorescent lights and any other lighting, the computer and any TV monitors

Your store – All animal-based materials (leather, wool, silk, bone, feathers, etc.), anything in the red color spectrum (oranges, pinks and all shades of red), art showing people, animals, sunshine, fire or bright illumination, triangles, pyramids, cone shapes, computers, TVs and all forms of lighting

Animals represent fire energy.

Earth

Vanilla box – Any squares or rectangles, large, flat surfaces, and bricks or ceramic tiles (if you're lucky)

Your store – Natural bricks or ceramic tiles where appropriate, adobe stucco, some yellow and earth tones, horizontal stripes, large and visually clean sheetrock ceiling, squares and rectangles represented by some of the fixtures

Terra cotta pots and any square tiles bring Earth energy into a space.

Metal

Vanilla box – Metal in the window frame, standards and studs in the walls

Your ideal store – All metals, rocks and stones including flagstone, granite, marble either on the walls or floors or in a sculpture, cement, natural crystals, white and pastel colors, circles, ovals and spheres

Natural crystals are powerful as a metal element as well as visually fascinating for your customers.

Each element brings something into your store that adds to the overall positive feel and energy:

- Water enhances introspection and inspiration.
- Wood encourages intuition and creativity.
- Fire ignites healthy emotional responses.
- Earth embraces sensuality and relaxation.
- The metal element strengthens mental perception.

Find the right proportion or balance of each element in your store. Too much or too little of one element can make a strong energetic difference, which can make shopping or work less comfortable.

- Too much wood can promote a sense of being overwhelmed, while too little can impede customers' ability to connect with your merchandise.
- Too much fire stimulates impatience and impulsive behavior, while too little is chilling and cuts down on friendly interactions.
- Too much earth creates an atmosphere that's overly serious or conservative, while too little promotes clutter, disorganization and a lack of clarity and sensuality.
- Too much metal creates mental rigidity, while too little encourages indecisiveness and procrastination.
- Too much water promotes spacey behavior and diminishes productivity, while too little creates stress and anxiety.

The study of the elements in Feng Shui goes into great depth about the Nourishing Cycle and the Controlling Cycle. The most important aspect of these cycles is to keep the elements balanced in the space.

Be Aware: Repetitive shapes such as urns, plates and photographs as well as monochromatic colors are part of good design, but they might result in an imbalance of elements. You can use the design elements of repetition and monochromatic colors, but make sure to add the missing elements through a combination of merchandise, props and a variety of natural surfaces to create a comfortable space for you, your staff and your customers.

Store Elements Analysis

Circle the elements you have in your store and add below any others that fit into the category above. Look to see if you have a balance in your store and if not, determine what you can add to create a more integrated, comfortable retail environment.

WOOD
Fixtures * plants/flowers * plant-based * cloth art/landscapes * plants/flowers * columnar shapes * paper

FIRE
Lighting * animal-based items * art/people/animals/sun/fire * triangles * red tones * natural sunlight * computer

EARTH
Adobe/brick/tile ceramics * squares/rectangles * yellow/earth tones * art/earthy landscapes * horizontal stripes

METAL
Any metals * cement/rocks/stones * natural crystals * art (metal or stone) * circles/ovals/arches * white/pastels

WATER
Fountain/fish tank * mirrors/glass/cut crystal * art/water scenes * freeform/free-flowing shapes * black/dark tones

Experiment with different combinations of elements and monitor the results. When specifically chosen for their elemental qualities, anything from wall color to a vase of flowers can add and balance missing elements and make your store instantly more appealing.

Yin and Yang

Imagine walking into a brightly lit store with each attractive focal display gleaming with light. You don't know where to look first because each area has its own beauty. As you walk through the store, you notice one dark, dim area, and this darkness seems to suck in all the surrounding light so that everything on its perimeter loses its identity. This dark area creates an imbalance in the store. This lack of balance in the light affects your entire perception of the store.

Balance is an essential element in our lives. All life is made up of two extremes and all that fall in between. In China, the two extremes are called Yin and Yang. Light and dark, wet and dry, sharp and curved, cold and warm are all polar opposites that work best when in balance with each other.

Yang is masculine. An all Yang store would be very bright and light with high ceilings, many large windows and lots of sharp angles in the fixtures and architecture. This store would initially be stimulating, but customers and sales staff would soon feel their energy diminish, as there would be no visual hiding or soft places.

Yin is feminine. An all Yin store would be dark, dim and cave-like with low ceilings, soft lighting and rounded shapes lacking definition. The fixtures would be crammed full of merchandise but it would be difficult to see because of the lack of light. This type of store could make people feel depressed by the darkness and a sense that the walls are closing in on them.

A successful store has a balanced combination of Yin and Yang. There is a pattern of light that ranges from soft to brighter to "pop." Rather than dark areas, there are small areas that are lit by task lighting such as fluorescents. These

YIN	YANG
Earth	Sky
Feminine	Masculine
Moonlight	Sunlight
Night	Day
Cool or cold	Warm or hot
Soft	Hard
Quiet	Noisy
Rounded	Angular
Low	High
Restful	Active
Small	Large
Ornate	Plain
Shady	Light
Dark	Bright
Curved	Straight
Yielding	Hard
Spiritual	Material
Emotional	Physical
Intuitive	Intellectual
Selfless	Self
Heart	Head
Wide	Narrow
Horizontal	Vertical
Floral	Geometrical
Back	Front
Student	Teacher

areas are balanced by other sections, which are highlighted by flood and spotlights. The fixtures have rounded edges that are easy to walk around, and the merchandise is well organized and attractively displayed.

The balanced store feels comfortable – it is neither too hot nor too cold, and fresh air is in constant circulation.

Case study #1:

An elegant store opened in a trendy shopping area of New York City. The store had a cement and mostly glass façade. The window area was very large. Inside, to the left, were two long rows of hanging white shirts with some shelves above. The right side of the store had some shelves with folded white shirts. The center area was bare and led to a back wall and stockroom. It was a brightly lit, hard-edged store selling white shirts to men.

The balance of Yin and Yang and of the elements was off. While the store was interesting looking, it was not a comfortable shopping experience. The open view into the store made the customers an integral part of the store's image and display. In fact, the customers were far more interesting than the all-white shirt merchandise. The store was very Yang. The bright lights, large, empty expanses, high ceiling, angled fixtures and spare merchandise all created a strong image, but not an appealing place to spend time. Although women purchase a good percentage of men's shirts, this store focused its energy on men alone. A woman will not feel comfortable in a totally Yang store. And most men will quickly start feeling uncomfortable as well.

The store closed in a short period of time. It needed more balance, some softer lighting, a more sensual feeling – some more Yin.

Case study #2:

The sales in the lingerie department of a well-known retailer were slipping rapidly. The balance of the Yin and Yang was completely off. Several important wall lights and focal spotlights had burned out as well as some fluorescent bulbs. Two areas within the department were dim and three wall displays were actually dark. The entire department felt dim and sad. The merchandise was disorganized and messy and felt neglected.

As soon as the lights were fixed, the entire energy of the space picked up and the salespeople felt compelled to clean up the clutter. Sales started improving immediately. It took two and a half weeks to get the lights fixed. Imagine how sales were affected in that time.

REVIEW

Chapter Two: The Balance of the Elements and Yin and Yang

1. For a human being to feel comfortable in a retail environment, the basic elements that are in nature and our bodies must be represented in the store and be in balance with each other.

2. The five elements are Water, Wood, Fire, Earth and Metal.
Water: *Introspection – Inspiration*
Intuition, communication, socializing, insightful. Still water = deep, introspective. Moving water = social, networking.

Wood: *Intuition – Creativity*
New ideas, beginnings, inspiration, optimism, expansion, unique, challenging, ambition, freedom from rules and obligations.
Fire: *Emotional Responses*
Intuitive, exciting, spontaneous, dramatic, intimacy and joy.
Earth: *Sensuality – Nurturing*
Nurturing, stabilizing and relaxing.
Metal: *Mental Perception*
Intense focus, ability to complete a sale, order, simplicity, efficiency, serenity, discernment, creativity and communication.

3. Each **element** must be represented in your store to achieve the balance needed for success.

4. If your store is unbalanced, the energy of you, your staff and the customers will wane over time, sales will diminish and the store will eventually close. Elements can be added through the **merchandise**, but don't rely solely on your merchandise to accomplish this task. Work with a store designer and your new knowledge of elements to create balance.

5. **Yang** is the masculine and refers to the nature of life energy, brightness, daylight and the sun. This is basically the life half of the Yin-Yang concept. Yang energy is symbolized by activity, bright lights, hardness and daytime hours. Yang is the white half of the yin/yang symbol.

6. **Yin** energy is the complete opposite of Yang energy. They never conflict but instead complement one another. They give life to each other and neither would exist without the other. Yin is darkness and silence, feminine and soft. Yin is the black half of the Yin/Yang symbol.

7. **Balance** between Yin and Yang is as important as the balance of the elements. A store that is too bright with hard surfaces will eventually tire the staff and customers. Equally, a store that is dark, comfortable and soft will tire people as well.

Store Balance Analysis for Yin and Yang

Use the following list to determine the current Yin/Yang balance of each room or major department of your store. This list can also be used for your home and office. If you have equal amounts of a feature, such as both small and large art, circle both. If there is a category that doesn't exist in a room, department or in the entire store, ignore it and move to the next one. If you have many departments or rooms in your store, make a copy of the form on the following two pages for each area.

With much thanks to:

Terah Kathryn Collins, *The Western Guide to Feng Shui: Room by Room,* The Hay House, 1999
Peggy Doscher, *Dynamic Feng Shui Master,* dynamicfengshui@hotmail.com
William Spear, *Feng Shui Made Easy,* HarperCollins, 1999
Lillian Too, *Lillian Too's Basic Feng Shui,* Oriental Publications, 1998

Name of Room or Department: ______________________

	YIN	YANG
Room size	small	large
Location in store	quiet/private	noisy/busy
Room's view	intimate/private	grand
Room's view	nature	houses/ buildings/ street
Ceiling	low	high
Natural light	low	bright
Electrical light	low	bright
Open floor space	small amounts	large expanses
Floors	carpeting/area	rugs/tile/ cement/wood/ stone
Wall colors	medium, dark or muted	light or bright
Fixtures & furniture	many pieces	few pieces
Fixture colors	medium, dark or muted	light or bright
Fixture sizes	small, medium	large, extra large
Fixture heights	low	high
Fixture shapes	curved, rounded lines and edges	straight, angular, sharp

---

With much thanks to

The Western School of Feng Shui: www.wsfs.com, 800-300-6785, 760-633-3388,
PO Box 946, Solana Beach, California 92075

	YIN	**YANG**
Seating	soft, padded	hard, unpadded
Patterns (i.e., walls/floors)	floral	geometric
Fabrics	textured	smooth/shiny
Store design	elaborate layered/ornate	simple/ uncomplicated
Displays	many	few or none
Art	many pieces	few or none
Art	small pieces	large pieces
Pillows/drapes/ fabric	many	few or none
Mirrors	small	large
Plants	many	few or none
Stockrooms/attic/ basement	organized	chaotic/ disorganized
TOTAL:	**YIN______**	**YANG_____**

In an ideal world, you will find an almost even balance between the Yin and Yang in your store. If the balance between the two is very different and your business is slow, or if you are not attracting or keeping the customers you desire, consider adding elements to create a better balance in your store.

3

Location. Location? Location!

The history and location of a store are two of the most important aspects of Feng Shui. Each will have an important influence on the future success of your store. How did the past owners do in this locale? Why did they leave? Was it to expand their space because they were doing so well or did they close because business was bad?

The preexisting energy in the space influences your store's present and future. This energy also applies if you have been in your space for a while but feel that your luck in the space hasn't been as good as you had originally hoped.

Positive History

- The storeowner wants to leave for a larger space.
- The storeowner wants to relocate and sell the store.
- The storeowner wants to retire.
- The storeowner's lease has run out and he is tired of the retail business. (This store will need reenergizing.)
- The storeowner is leaving the business because of a marriage or birth.
- The storeowner is a large corporation that is closing some of its stores.

Negative History

- The storeowner went bankrupt.
- Stores all around the one you're interested in are going out of business.
- There was a lot of illness and absenteeism.
- The owner closed the store due to poor business.
- There was a murder on the street in front of or in the store.
- There was a suicide in the store. (If someone passed away at the store, that's a part of life – but murder and suicide are very negative and the vibrations last a long time.)

Unless you build a store from the ground up, you will have to work with the influences from the past owners. With luck, these influences will be positive. But, if your store has a negative past, you will want to take the following steps.

Remedies for Negative History

1. Find a Feng Shui master or respected practitioner in your area and ask him or her to do a space clearing and to clean the store's energy for you. This is worth the money. Do not

have a psychic clean the energy through candles or crystals. Although some of these people are excellent, a good Feng Shui practitioner will see what needs to be done to "cure the space" rather than just clean out stuck spirits.

2. Look at the alignment of the doors of the store. If your front door and back door are aligned, your money might come in the front and flow out the back. Build a wall 3 feet in front of the back door and use it as a focal display area. Light it well with spotlights to draw attention to the merchandise rather than the stockroom door. If you can't build a wall, hang a piece of heavy fabric 3 feet in front of the stockroom door and put a tiered table display in front. The basic idea here is to hide the stockroom door and to block the energy from the front door from flowing easily out the back.

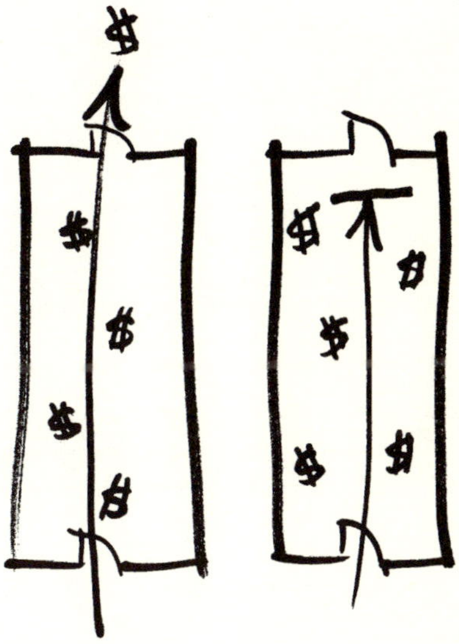

Front and Back doors aligned = Bad Luck! Build a floor-ceiling 4-foot wide wall in front of the back door = Good Luck!

3. Sprinkle sea salt all around the perimeter of your store and say a prayer that the energy of your store be cleansed of any negativity and loss.

4. Buy a new cash register and office desk. Do not use the register or desk from a failed business.

5. You can reuse fixtures from a failed store, but they must be *thoroughly* cleaned, repaired and moved into new areas.

6. Write your intention for the store's future on a piece of paper and mount it on a wall where you and your staff can see it daily. Make the intention powerful by using only positive words and stating it in the present tense. For example: *This store is filled with customers every day who love to shop here and who happily purchase and keep lots of merchandise. Our customers return frequently because they enjoy the store and are always asking, "What's new?" and we are showing them our new merchandise. We are successful and we enjoy our customers, our environment and our jobs.*

Please note that the customers "purchase and keep" lots of merchandise rather than the negative thought form "purchase and don't return" lots of merchandise. Keeping all your intentions in a positive form will greatly enhance the power of this affirmation or intention.

Unfortunate Street Locations

If your store has a negative past, it might have negative energy externally. This is where "location, location, location" comes into play. There are some locations that are considered very unfortunate in terms of Feng Shui.

Cul-de-Sac

A cul-de-sac is never good for a home and is only marginally good for a retail store. The energy circulates in a cul-de-sac like a whirlwind and shards of energy spin off the whirlwind and hit the homes or stores. This is a disturbing and energetically negative form of energy and causes a lack of harmony in the home/store or in the development area. Cars can easily spin out of control in a cul-de-sac and hit a home or storefront.

Cure: Planting trees or placing boulders in the potential path of speeding automobiles is the first step in making this configuration safer. Don't plant or place anything directly in front of your doorway. It is still vital that energy is able to enter your store without blocks. Another cure is to offset lights on the property of the store (or home) to divert the energy to a safer spot.

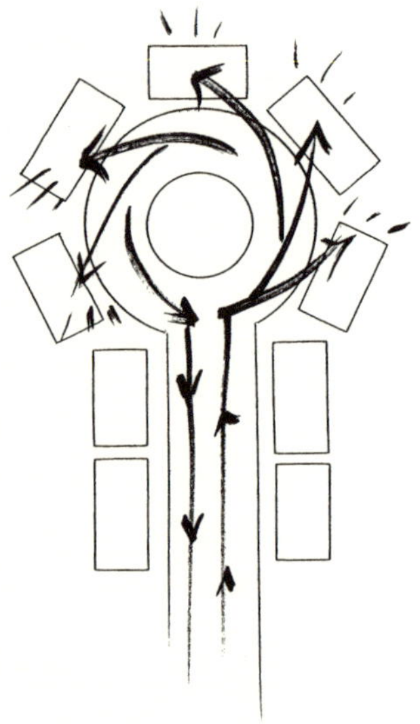

Cul-de-sacs can create confusion and discord.

At the End of a Long Hallway in an Enclosed Mall

Energy travels quickly down straight hallways and gets trapped at the end. This is called "angry energy" as it has no place to move so it rushes through your open doors. This "angry energy" may cause disagreements and arguments among you, your staff and customers. It also can create a feeling of being trapped with nowhere to go in life.

Cure: Move! If you can't move, develop a circular planting area in front of your store to slow the energy down before it hits your store. Of course, most malls will not allow you to do this without torturing you for months. But if you offer to have them speak with a local Feng Shui expert, they might change their minds. It's sometimes easier to fix a problem than to find a new tenant. If you haven't been paying your rent on time they may, however, prefer to find a new tenant.

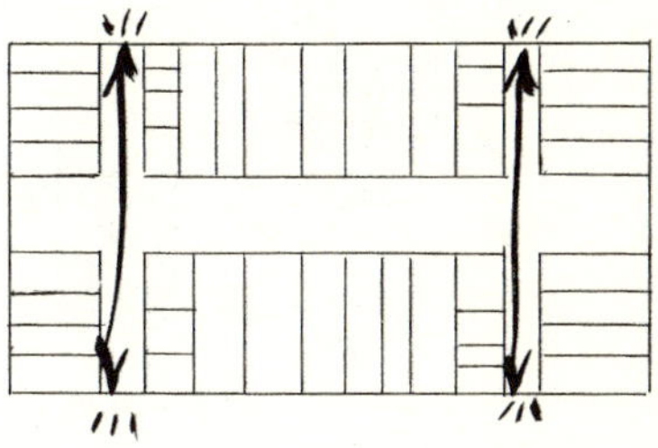

Trapped energy at the end of dead-end aisles in malls.

At the End of a T-Intersection

While being at the end of a T-intersection provides great visibility to your store, it also means a huge amount of energy is rushing toward – and into – your front door. This can feel very uncomfortable to anyone standing in the entrance area.

Cure: Create a protective barrier between your store and the street. Make sure it doesn't block people from coming into your front door but will deflect cars from driving through if they fail to stop at the intersection. Two effective cures are a 3-foot-high stone or brick wall or large concrete planters with evergreens. Install bright, attractive lights at either end of your building's façade. This will help deflect negative energy from the entrance area.

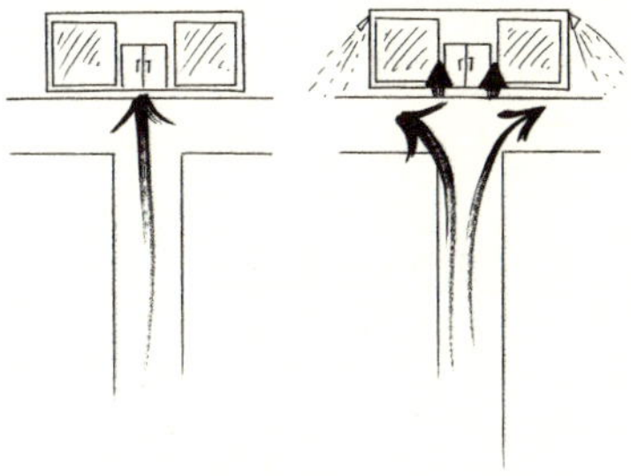

Distract rushing energy at the end of a T-intersection with cement planters and lights at the ends of your building.

Sandwiched Between Two Taller Buildings

Two taller buildings will draw energy from the middle, smaller one while unleashing downward energy onto the lower store. This is known as "a child between two bullies."

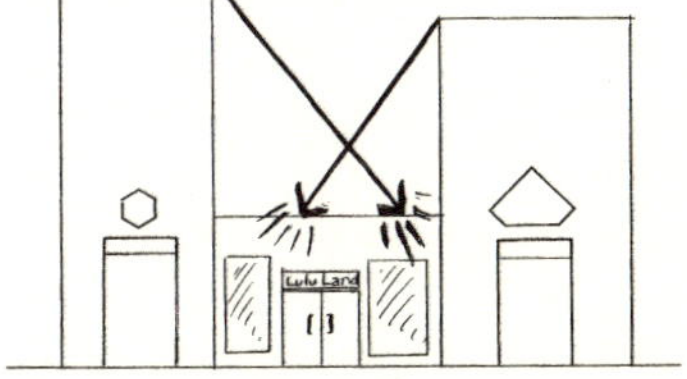

"Child between two bullies."

Add a flag, plants or bagua mirrors and shine extra light on your front sign.

Cure: Put a flagpole on top of your building with your store's name or logo emblazoned on the large flag. Add extra lighting to the store name above your entrance. If you can add potted trees on your roof – even better. Place two Bagua mirrors on the roof reflecting the buildings on either side. Make sure they are angled so they can't reflect sunlight, to avoid causing a fire!

Poison Arrows

Poison arrows are angles that point toward your store in the form of strongly slanted rooflines; the edges or corners of buildings, or buildings with their angles pointing to your façade; angled rooftops that aim toward your roof; or any other protruding architectural elements (street sign, banner pole) that "hit" your store like a knife.

Cure: This is where a Bagua mirror really comes in handy. Position it over your doorway to reflect the offending poison arrow back to its source. If the reflection on the mirror "hits" the entrance of the store across the street, you will reflect the negative energy back to them and their luck will start to fail. What goes around comes around. No one should fail in order for you to succeed. There's enough wealth for everyone to feel comfortable.

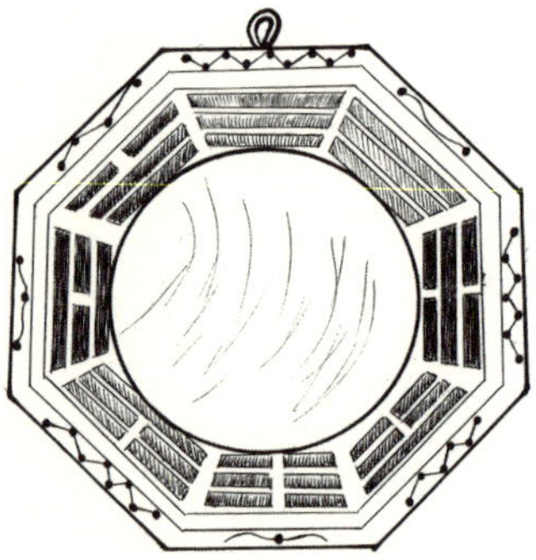

Bagua concave mirror.

If you are in a location with one of these problems and your business is doing well and all is good in your life – don't worry about it. There might be other, more powerful, positive influences that are affecting your business in a wonderful way.

If things are not going well and there is conflict, strife, negativity, very slow business, lots of anxiety, problems at home or ill health, start working on the cure for your location.

Mall Locations and Their Remedies

Some malls are designed with no real main doors. This is considered to be very negative Feng Shui. It is vital for customers to know where to walk into the mall for the energy or chi to flow smoothly.

In a mall location, make sure your store faces as much "empty" or clear space as possible. When your store faces the wall of a narrow corridor, the energy trying to enter your store becomes compressed and restrained.

A successful pushcart tenant at an upscale mall was given the option to move into a temporary store location on a busy floor. She jumped at the chance but within two weeks, a Kia was parked directly in front of her entrance, blocking both the view of her store and the energy flow from entering. Her once booming business became stagnant and while she drew in her existing loyal customers, it was difficult to attract new ones. She didn't know that the space in front of her store was leased to the car dealership. If you are leasing a space in a mall, make sure you know what will be in front of your store. The more space the better to attract people into your shop.

Plants or softly flowing banners add extra energy in a long hallway.

Customers rarely want to walk down narrow hallways in malls, and those locations are highly undesirable, which is why they are less expensive. If you are stuck in one of these hallways, negotiate for your signage to be perpendicular to the front of your store so that customers can see your name from the beginning of the hallway. Find out if it is possible to "break" your lease line with some potted plants on rollers or a sculptural item that reflects your store's merchandise and image. For example, if you have a restaurant, place a menu board out front or a fiberglass or wood chef holding the menu for all to see.

A manicure shop opened at the end of a "dead" corridor in a mall in Southern California. The owner was familiar with Feng Shui and hung banners outside her entrance to announce her location. The banners attracted customers who could see from a distance that there was a manicure shop at the end of the long, dark hall. The mall management insisted that the owner remove the banners, which she did, unhappily. Her business dropped and she immediately put out a sandwich board. This helped draw in new customers until the mall insisted that it be removed. The banners went back up until they were noticed by management and were then removed. The game continued and possibly is still going on today. The owner knew what she was doing and decided to be disliked rather than go out of business.

Important tip: Try to add strong lights to your façade and even have it "pour out" of your front door to claim the space in front of your store. People are attracted to light and will perceive it as leading them into the store. Continue this effect by making sure the interior lighting gets stronger as customers move into the store. It should be very bright in the rear of the store to pull people further into the space.

Case Studies

When a strong, successful chain store moves into a "negative" space, there might be no need to clean the energy. There was a combination health food store and restaurant in a strip mall in a medium-sized town in the Northeast. It was very popular for many years but due to poor management and high prices, combined with the opening of Trader Joe's next door, the retailer's packaged food business started to fail, as well as its vitamin business. Trader Joe's carried a lot of the same brands plus their own excellent vitamins at half the price.

The energy seemed to seep out of the health food store. While the restaurant continued to prosper, the energy of the store weakened. As the energy weakened, it affected the restaurant area and people started to feel uncomfortable and depressed. Eventually, the health food store stopped paying its bills and was evacuated. Trader Joe's expanded into the space physically – just as it had energetically. It was so strong that the weaknesses of the smaller store were magnified.

One option that might have given the smaller retailer a fighting chance was to expand and advertise its food bar/restaurant and quickly remove the vitamin and packaged food business. Then, find a tenant in a complementary business to lease the unused space. Instead, they held on in the hopes that people would remain loyal, but over time, low prices won.

The lesson of this story is that when a larger, more powerful store moves in next door and carries the same or similar merchandise for lower prices, you need to either change your merchandise selection quickly – and being smaller, you can react swiftly – or you can fail. There are very few options to this scenario. No amount of good Feng Shui will counteract a powerful chain of stores with lower prices. This is where your intention becomes vital.

When you find out that a big, powerful, competitive store is moving next to you (or close by), you can rant, rave, cry and give up, or you can rethink, renew, refresh, reinvent and stay in business. It's up to you.

A thriving two-story restaurant and bar closed its doors after 26 years in business, and the owners happily and comfortably retired. A different restaurant with excellent food leased the location, but redesigned the upper level to become the restaurant because the sloped driveway made it easier to enter through the top floor from the parking lot. The new owners completely ignored the ground-floor level, which used to be an active and popular singles bar. The windows on the ground floor used to be alive with lights but became dark and empty when it was converted to storage and office space.

This restaurant stayed in business for one year before closing and turning its lease over to a different restaurant owner, who proceeded to make the same mistake as the previous owner: leaving the windows empty and soulless. Two more restaurants opened and closed within a five-year period and the location developed the reputation of being "unlucky." It was certainly lucky for the original owners, who energized their upstairs restaurant with a popular bar below. This flourishing energy "propped up" and supported the upstairs.

If you have two floors, make sure your windows on both levels tell your customers who and what you are. Keep them well lit during the hours you are open for business. Don't leave one floor empty to suck the life out of the other. If you only want your store to be on one level, make your lower or upper level positive, cared for and a constructive part of the overall store plan.

Elliot Jay Tanzer, author of *Choose the Best House for You: The Feng Shui Checklist* (Elliot Jay Tanzer, 2003), is a cofounder of the Integrative School of Feng Shui and has lectured frequently around the United States. He has extensively studied many of the schools of Feng Shui and is an expert on locations and cures.

Tips from Elliot Jay Tanzer

1. It is more favorable to locate a place of business on the inside bend of a road than on the outside bend (similar to the cul-de-sac idea). Homes or businesses on the outside bend feel the continual intimidation of the cars driving toward them, which may in fact lose control. Even though no car does, the anxiety pervades.

Symbolically, it also represents, and comes to be, that money comes quickly to the store and then just as quickly leaves. Businesses on the outside bend tend to be less secure, less prosperous and always hungry for business.

2. Use the Black Sect alignment of the Wealth Area of the Eight Aspirations being located in the far left corner from the front door of the store or the Southeast for the Compass School of Feng Shui. As this area psychologically comes to symbolize the Wealth Area, avoid a location that has the bathroom situated here, as the money will go down the toilet. Bathrooms situated in any other corner can usually be balanced as long as the bathroom is kept clean and pleasant. Appropriate posters or colors can be used to counterbalance the excessive water element energy and the draining of energy often associated with the bathroom. If the bathroom is being used as a storage closet, keep all supplies, mops, vacuums, etc., in cabinets or at least behind a curtain. It is also advisable to avoid locations that have the bathroom in the center of the establishment, as illnesses are likely, especially flu's and viruses. If necessary, at least paint the walls a pale yellow or any other earth tone, and keep it clean and in good working order.

3. If the entranceway door opens outward (many fire codes require this), make sure the door is hinged so it opens to welcome the flow of foot traffic and not against it.

REVIEW

Chapter Three: Location. Location? Location!

1. The **preexisting** energy in a store influences both the present and future of your business.

2. If the store has a **negative past**, you will need to do a space clearing. Some methods for clearing include: prayer, sprinkling salt in all the corners, smoking with cedar and sage, and hiring a Feng Shui consultant to help clear the space.

3. If the store is at the end of a **T-intersection**, divert the rushing energy with lights on either end of your storefront and block the flow of energy with attractive plantings, using cement planters on either side of your front door.

4. Don't use cashwrap/desks or registers from **failed businesses**. Energetically clean the fixtures.

5. Keep the **doorway clear** of obstacles both outside and inside the store.

6. If you are in a **dead-end corridor** in a mall, add extra lights at your entrance to throw light out into the mall. Make sure your store glows to attract attention.

7. Become aware of **poison arrows** coming from other buildings surrounding your store. If a corner of a building is pointing at your store, consider mounting a Bagua mirror to deflect the negative energy. Bagua mirrors are very powerful and must be used with caution as they can either start fires if they reflect the sun onto flammable materials or they can hurt a neighbor's business.

8. Try to find a space in a mall or on the street that has as much **empty space** in front of your door as possible. This empty space welcomes in energy and allows it to flow easily into your store.

9. Your **windows** reflect the soul of your store. If you have windows that can be seen from the street, in the basement or above your store, fill them with images or products that reflect your image and purpose. Empty windows will eventually create empty stores.

10. If the **entranceway door** opens outward, make sure the door is hinged so it opens to welcome the flow of foot traffic and not against it.

4

First Impressions

Basics for Store Entrances

Imagine you're walking down a busy street. You are aware of all the people walking next to you and toward you. The people coming toward you are in your immediate sightline, and unconsciously you size up each person within a fraction of a second. In that moment, you determine whether they are safe, strange or fabulous. The safe people quickly disappear from your conscious mind. You tend to stare more at the strange or fabulous people. The strange people are instantly analyzed for their danger potential, while the fabulous people will get your full attention because watching them is just plain fun!

Is your store façade safe? Is it strange? Is it fabulous? Your storefront creates an immediate and lasting impression of the store – for better or for worse.

Your storefront tells your potential customers if they belong in your store. It acquaints people with your merchandise message. It also might relate the wrong message. Feng Shui defines your main door as the blessings area where luck – both good and bad – flows into your store. Not only does your façade need to create the proper image to attract your perfect customers, but it also needs to welcome in good luck and repel negativity.

First, from a good visual merchandising point of view, make sure your façade and signage match your desired image. If you have a very upscale store and your façade matches your interior, you're ahead of the game. If you are in an old, beat-up building but desire an upscale customer, you have your work cut out for you. Don't assume customers will overlook a run-down façade. Your building front, whether you are upscale, mainstream or discount, must be clean, freshly painted or power washed, easily accessible, well lit and preferably have some greenery or flowers in front to welcome and soften your entrance. Your store name, sign font style, color and shape tell customers who and what you are. This is not always a good thing!

When a family decides to open a store together, what often results is a store created by a committee. When the most forceful, whiny or anxious member of the family pushes an idea, it might be difficult to reject. An upscale women's clothing store recently opened with its sign logo in hot pink bubble letters – a particular favorite of the middle child in the family. Hot pink bubble letters say "teenage customer." This combination also indicates affordability – not upscale women's clothing. The retailer is still trying to find its customer before the money runs out.

Entrances Do's and Don'ts

- Make sure nothing is blocking people from entering your store. This includes trees, architectural barriers and steep or uneven steps.
- Don't clutter the entrance. Keep it open and clear for customers to easily walk in without having to negotiate sign holders, dump tables or curled-up floor mats.
- Floor mats are great, but make sure they are flush to the floor and don't shift or move underfoot.
- Be aware that people will tend to move in the direction your floor mat is pointing. "Play" with the placement of the mat until it feels like your store is expansive rather than narrow.

Expansive floor mat placement.

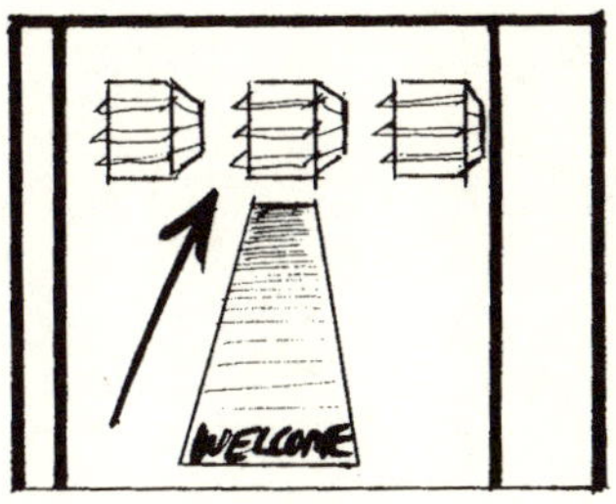

Directional floor mat.

You can say welcome, but don't have people walk on your name.

- Light up the front of your store as well as inside the entrance. People are attracted to light, and a light in the entrance area adds positive Yang energy and attracts good energy into your store. It pays to leave some entrance lights on all night as well. In this way, the entrance area never becomes stagnant. Look into full-spectrum fluorescent bulbs for your entryway fixtures so you can keep your heat and electrical costs down.
- If you have your own parking lot, the image and identity of your store extend into that lot. That means your store colors should wrap around your store into the lot as well as your signage wherever possible. Adding trees, evergreens, flowers and grassy areas will enhance the positive energy coming into your store. Make sure the parking lot is brightly lit for safety as well as good Feng Shui. If you have room out front, consider the addition of a small bench and a stable, clean, well-maintained trashcan with a covered sand area on top for cigarette butts.

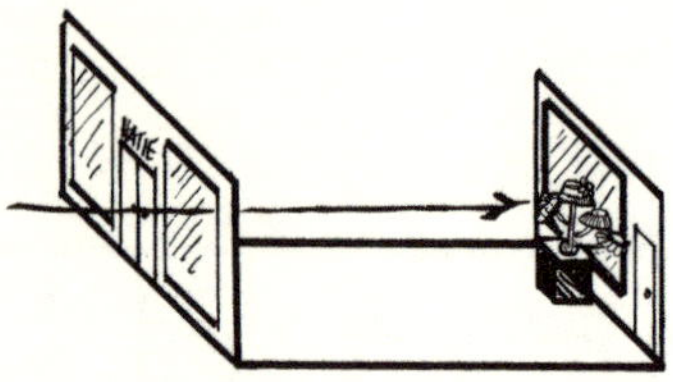

Windows aligned — with a display to stop the energy.

- If a customer can see through your front windows and door straight through a window in the back, you will be losing energy in your store. The simple remedy for this is to add a Yin balancing element. A sheer curtain, a beautiful display or a high table or fixture arrangement that blocks the energy between the front and back windows will do the trick.
- Window displays need to reflect your image in a professional manner. If you do not have the time or talent to create appropriate window displays, hire someone who does. Consider that person a vital part of your advertising budget. The window displays will pay for themselves quickly. Before the first display installation, discuss your store's image, merchandise and advertising concepts with the visual merchandiser. Discuss different ideas and don't be afraid to push the envelope a bit. Look at how going beyond the expected benefited Barneys! If your visual merchandiser is going in the wrong direction, bring him back to your reality. If you like and trust the person, it's worth taking the time to learn to work together.

Best Front Door Colors

Certain colors enhance the energy in each direction. Your front door painted the right color will augment your store's luck. Paint your door according to the direction it faces:
South – red, green or brown
Southwest – orange or red
Southeast – green, blue or black
North – black, blue or white
Northwest – metallic, white or yellow
Northeast – red, blue or orange
West – metallic, white or yellow
East – green, blue or black

You can use different tones of any of these colors. Your intention is what matters! If you prefer not to have a red door, you can use burgundy, cranberry or shades of pink.

You might have only a glass door to work with rather than wood or metal. You can bring your lucky color into your canopy instead of painting the door. If you prefer not to use this color, consider flowers or a flowerpot in your lucky color next to your front door and fill it either with seasonal plantings or with an evergreen. Red attracts prosperity but is best when used sparingly and with intention.

Front Door Tips

Oversized doors.

The larger the door, the wider the opening – the more chi and luck can flow into your store.

- If the door is too heavy or large to open easily, the luck will be reversed. If the front door is out of proportion to the rest of the façade, it takes away from the overall positive first impression.
- It is considered to be very lucky when a front door faces a wide street, sidewalk, open space or bright area.
- You might be able to energetically create that open space in a mall by asking that benches and any moveable objects in front of your entrance be moved away from your front door. This might also work in a town or city (depending on the bureaucracy).
- A small bell or nicely tuned wind chime on your front door helps to energize the entrance and welcome in good luck.
- Banners or any other moving objects that work with the image and identity of your store are an excellent way to attract positive attention as well as welcome energy into your store.

Outside banners create excitement.

- Try not to have mirrors reflect your entrance, staircases or restrooms. If they do, make sure there is merchandise between the mirror and the door, stairwell or toilet so the merchandise is reflected first. Ideally, the mirrors should reflect the cash register if that is a viable option.
- Bring your lucky color into your window displays whenever possible. This can be done with props, pads on the walls or floors, signage or actual merchandise. Of course, you need to change your windows at the very least every two weeks, and the colors will change along with the windows. Don't worry if your lucky color isn't in your windows week after week. Use it with intent when you want a little jump-start for your business.

Best scenario — lots of space in front of your store with good lights.

Entering the Store – First Impressions

Your façade, windows, signage and plantings have set the stage. What is the customers' instant first impression as they enter your store? The entry area is where people have a chance to stop and survey their surroundings. This area should be clear of any obstructions and floor level changes. If you are using a floor mat, realize that it is a great opportunity to enhance your décor. It can be fun and colorful if that works for your image.

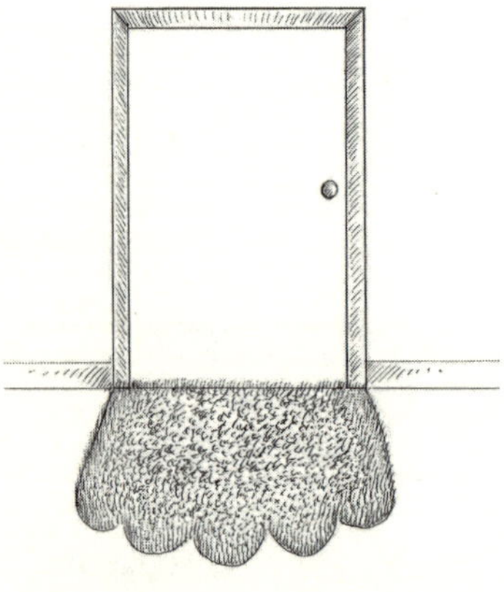

Pre-teens will appreciate fun doormats like this one cut from indoor/outdoor grass matting.

For example, a terrific store geared to teenage girls used fake indoor/outdoor grass cut into the shape of a hand for its entry mat. It was fun and highly creative. The floor mat also directs people to some part of your store. Move the front mat until it makes the store feel more welcoming and spacious. Naturally, it should be flat on the floor with slip-proof rubber underneath (if needed) to keep it safe. Holes, tears and curled edges create a poor first impression and are a danger to your customers.

A gift shop in Connecticut had a classic rectangular layout. It was wide rather than deep, and its entrance rug pointed directly to the front row of fixtures. Although visually this was great for those fixtures, it made the configuration of the store feel narrower and limited. We turned the rug so it ran horizontal or parallel to the front door, and the store immediately felt wider. Customers began to move in a different pattern when they entered. Rather than walking straight ahead to the first row of fixtures, they veered left and worked their way around the entire store.

Entrance Tips from Terah Kathryn Collins

In an article for *New Age Retailer* magazine, Collins perfectly summed up Feng Shui entryways:

Great Feng Shui honors and satisfies the instinctual needs for safety, comfort, beauty and positive change. An irresistible atmosphere begins at your front door, where first impressions are saying, "Yes" or "No" to potential customers. Your task is to create an especially welcoming front entrance area so the impression is always "Yes." The following mistakes, commonly made by storeowners, tend to elicit a "No" response and push customers away before they can enter the store:

- Tall display shelves located near the front entrance. Instinct says, "Danger, I can't see what's behind that abrupt rise."
- Too much merchandise arranged around the entrance. Even when it's attractive, instinct warns, "Too much stimulation. I can't take all this in right now."
- Shelves, counters or furniture with sharp corners that point directly toward the front entrance. Instinct says, "Danger, there's an arrow pointed right at me!"

Here's where you can employ some classic Feng Shui. Visualize your store's front entrance area as the floor of a valley. About 8 feet inside the door, the first low "hill" or display rises. Designed to be the "greeter," it's decidedly welcoming and communicates complete safety and allure. This could be a table or area that includes soft detailing such as fabric, upholstered items, plants or flowers that do not block the view into the store.

Ideally, there are two pathways around it that are 4 or 5 feet wide so that two customers can walk side by side or pass each other with ease. The various displays then rise incrementally higher as they move back into the store. This "command view over rising hills" from the front entrance, as well as the ease of passage into the store, is very compelling to shoppers as they instinctively respond to the inviting landscape of your store.

Add to this an especially attractive display in the center of the store and shoppers are drawn in to explore the heart of the space. High shelves and other displays can act as beauty marks and define the outer boundary around the perimeter of the store. In larger stores, they can be used to embellish and define sub-areas within the space. The point is to create a commanding and very inviting view into the store from the front entrance.

REVIEW

Chapter Four: First Impressions

1. Your storefront tells your potential customers if they belong in your store. It acquaints people with your **merchandise message.**

2. From a good visual merchandising point-of-view, make sure your façade and signage match your **desired image.**

3. Make sure **nothing is blocking** people from entering your store. This includes trees, architectural barriers and steep or uneven steps.

4. **Don't clutter** the entrance. Keep it open and clear for customers to walk in easily, without having to negotiate sign holders, dump tables or curled-up floor mats.

5. **Light up** the front of your store as well as inside the entrance. People are attracted to light, and a light in the entrance area adds positive Yang energy.

6. If you have your own **parking lot**, the image and identity of your store extends into that lot. Make sure your store's image and identity is consistent on the exterior.

7. Energy will escape through your store if the **front window aligns** with a back window. Two remedies are hanging a faceted crystal in one of the windows and creating an attractive display or merchandise presentation to block the back window.

8. The larger the **door**, the wider the opening – the more chi and luck can flow into your store. If the door is too heavy or large to open easily, the luck will be reversed. If the front door is out of proportion to the rest of the façade, it takes away from the overall positive first impression.

9. **Banners** or any other moving objects that work with the image and identity of your store are an excellent way to attract positive attention as well as welcome energy into your store.

10. Your **window displays** tell customers who you are, what you sell and who you think they are. If the displays are highly visible, they become your most powerful form of advertising. Either find the time to do them well or hire someone whose work you respect to install new windows for you every three weeks. If you are in a metropolitan area, every two weeks is better.

First Impressions Survey

This is a quick survey that you can give to your associates, family and favorite customers. Try to get at least five people to fill out this survey. You will be surprised with the results. Once you become aware of what people are seeing and feeling as they enter your store, you will have an action plan for visual merchandising and Feng Shui cures and enhancements.

1. What are the first three things you see as you walk up to the store?

    1.
    2.
    3.

2. What is your immediate feeling about the store?

3. What is your first impression of the store?

4. Who do you feel is the right type of customer for this store?

5. Is it easy to walk into the store, or are you blocked in some way from entering effortlessly?

____

____

6. What are the first five things you see as you enter the store?

1.
2.
3.
4.
5.

7. Which way do you want to walk?

____

8. How does the front of the store feel?

9. Once in the store, how does the store feel?

10. How do you feel in the store?

5

Feng Shui and the Selling Floor

Everyone shops with his or her own unique style. Some people stop in the front entrance and read a store from left to right as if it's a book before venturing into the interior. Others march right up to the first fixture and stay there until they determine whether to move further into the store. Still others walk in, look at the first fixture and walk right out again. Those last types are pretty scary for a retailer. Use Feng Shui in your floor plans to help those scary customers decide to flow into your store rather than walk away.

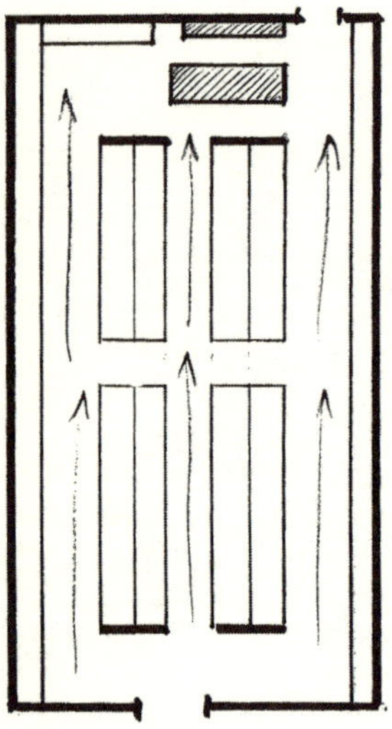

Long, straight aisles send people and energy rushing to the back of the store — missing merchandise on the way.

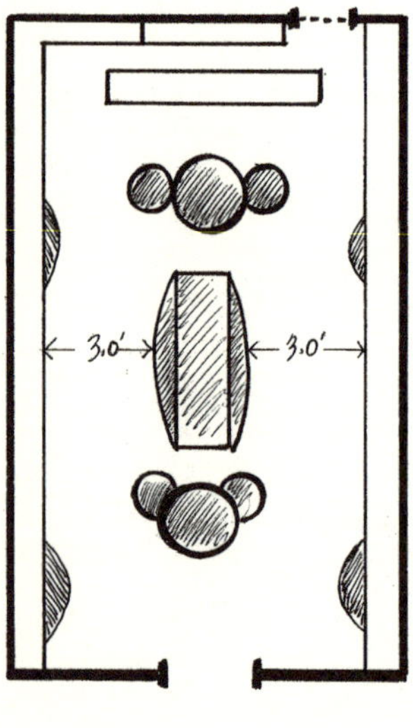

Create displays and merchandise presentations in the center of a narrow store.

Create the Best Traffic Pattern for Your Store

Whether a store is large or small, the best traffic patterns, according to Feng Shui, avoid long, straight aisles. Energy flows swiftly down straight paths – and so do customers. When you look at the success of Wal-Mart, Target, Best Buy, Home Depot, Lowe's and the office supply chains – Office Depot, Staples and Office Max – you might wonder if this aspect of Feng Shui is out to lunch.

The longer and straighter the aisle, the more quickly energy will flow to the end. In Feng Shui, this has always been considered a negative. Why this works for some big-box stores and not for others depends upon many variables. Wal-Mart has long aisles with departments on either side of the aisles. The main aisles are energy pathways that defy traditional Feng Shui rules for one main reason: These main aisles are so wide that quite often "special purchases" or dump tables are positioned in their centers. This immediately changes the traffic flow and creates interesting pods of merchandise. Rather than rush down the aisle to get to their destination department, customers slow down to check out the specials in the aisles.

The other successful big-box retailers do this as well. Home Depot, an extremely busy store, does not, but the ladders, the boxes on the floor, pallets and carts left in the aisles accomplish the same thing – just in a more irritating manner. Rushing down an aisle at Home Depot is more fantasy than reality.

Some of the most successful specialty retailers in the United States have more circuitous floor plans. Gap Inc., The Limited and Pier One all require the customer to navigate in a serpentine flow though their floor fixtures. Each time a customer turns, he sees a new merchandise story on an angled fixture. Shopping those stores is more of a visual treat and adventure. In terms of energy flow, these serpentine aisles allow energy – and people – to flow more comfortably through a store.

Circular aisle plan.

Many years ago, Saks Fifth Avenue in New York City was redesigned and renovated with a circular floor plan on each floor. This successful aisle plan is still in use and has influenced countless other retailers. At Saks, a customer can turn either right or left as he comes out of the elevators or off the escalator onto a selling floor. As he walks, he encounters shallow departments, each telling a merchandise or vendor story. As he travels around the circular "racetrack" floor, he stays longer and sees more because rather than endless aisles of fixtures, there are instead softly curved aisles with strong focal areas at every turn. Once he makes it halfway around the circle, it makes more sense to keep going around the floor to see everything rather than turn around to retrace his steps.

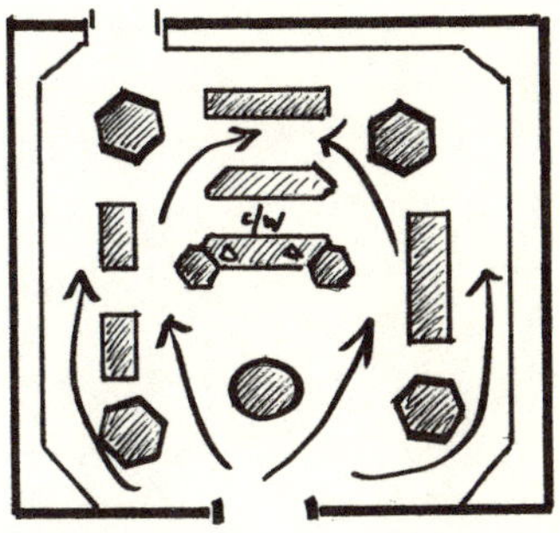
Square store.

This aisle plan introduced new departments to customers who were stuck in their shopping patterns. In terms of Feng Shui, a cul-de-sac roadway might not be great for a home site, but an interior cul-de-sac can be excellent for a retail environment. The energy that moves around curved aisles in a store is softer and slower. Having this energy spin off and hit a department is a good thing as this energy pulls in customers. The center of the selling floor becomes dressing rooms – the center of balance and sales for a soft-line store. In a hard-line store, the center of the store can be an information/sales desk or the most popular merchandise classification.

Long store, serpentine aisles.

This "racetrack" aisle plan has been picked up by many different types of retailers and is excellent for almost all merchandise categories. When you visualize the Bagua

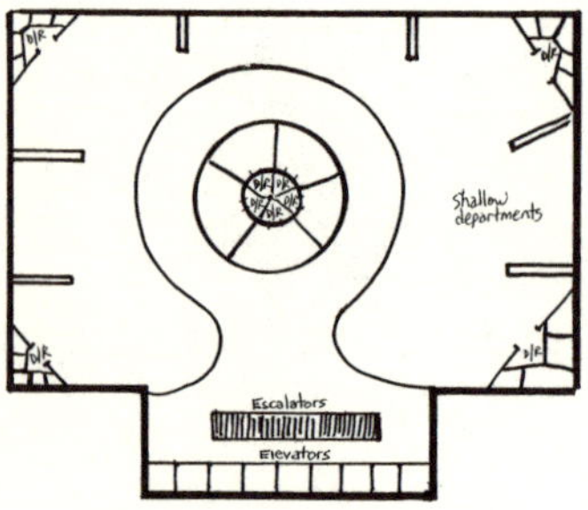

Based on the NYC Saks Fifth Avenue basic selling floor plan.

map, remember that the center of balance and health is in the center ninth of the store. This is the core balance area of the store and is not the place for toilets or stairwells – especially circular. This center area is acceptable for cash registers but is most appropriate for a department or merchandise that best represents your store's image, concept and values.

Decompression Zone

Every store needs an entrance area where a customer can stand for a moment and size up the store. From this safe spot, he scans the store to get an idea of the merchandise selection, if it looks interesting and in which direction to walk to start shopping. This area is called "the decompression zone."

When a store is short on space and there is a perceived need to fill every square foot with merchandise, the decompression zone is often the first area to get filled. This is not a great idea. If a person stops at your entrance and what they see on that first fixture isn't to her liking, she's going to walk away. If you must add merchandise in the valuable decompression area, try to create a low, tiered display with a strong color story and a good mix of merchandise.

If you sell hardware, this might be the best spot for a seasonal display. In the summer it's barbecues and all related products, while in winter it becomes snow shovels, blowers and bags of ice melt in many parts of the country. If you sell soft goods, this decompression area should be as lightly fixtured as possible. Open with a low, tiered table arrangement with a bright or black/white and bright color story. If you sell accessories, it pays to create a display on the top tier with a piece of merchandise combined with matching accessories so customers can see immediately what you have to offer further back in the store. Yes, the accessories might be stolen. Use pins, double-stick tape or whatever it takes to slow down a shoplifter.

The low fixtures are the key to both of these presentations. If you visually block a prospective customer so he can't see a good part of the store, he might feel uncomfortable entering. Our animal instincts tell us not to enter a cave without knowing what's living inside. While our sophisticated intellect tells us a store is safe, the ancient animal in us is looking for the paths in and out before entering. The other reason to have low fixtures is for the sales staff's benefit. The more they can see, the better their service will be, combined with reduced theft.

The owner of a women's clothing store in New York's Greenwich Village called me because his business was dying and he didn't know why. Almost every customer who walked into the store stopped, briefly looked at a rack of clothing and walked right out again. When I arrived, I watched women walk in, look at the rolling rack at the front door, turn around and leave. I immediately moved the rack out of the front door area. We then angled all the floor fixtures so customers could see a large selection of merchandise when glancing around the store. Rather than having the bright colors mixed in with the ubiquitous blacks, grays and browns, we put them in the most visible locations to brighten up the feel of the store. Color attracts and inspires sales. Dark colors sell better when surrounded by bright tones.

Fixture blocking entry.

The basic problem was that the rack in the front of the store was defining the entire store's merchandise selection. If a woman walked in and didn't like what was on that front rack, she left the store. The rolling rack itself was blocking energy from flowing easily into the store. Once the fixture

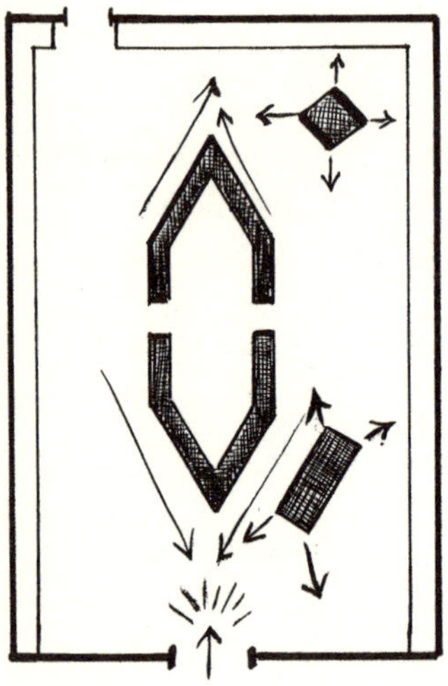

Poison arrows coming off points on diamond, square and rectangular fixtures.

Irritating fixtures with sharp points.

Sharp pointed fixtures pointing towards customers as they enter the front door.

was moved to the side, customers could see a wide range of merchandise all over the store and their buying options expanded.

Poison Arrows

Poison arrows are created by energy flowing swiftly down sharp angles that are found on fixtures, walls and ceilings. Imagine a cashwrap desk designed so it points toward the front door.

As you walk into the store, the corner acts like the point of a knife aiming for your midsection. This is not a pleasant sensation. While these angles make for good retail drama, remember that many dramas are uncomfortable and usually involve some pain. Whenever a person feels like she has to be careful shopping a store, she is less comfortable and will stay for less time. If your salespeople have poison arrows pointing at them daily, they will start feeling ill and irritable. They will unconsciously move away from the point to a more desirable location. Your customers will do the same. If the arrow points to an important focal area in your store, you will lose sales in that area.

An upscale women's specialty shop opened in an affluent town about 50 miles outside of New York City. The store's angled counters were designed like chevrons with the corner of the first counter pointing like an arrow to the midsection of all who entered the store. Within a day, a salesperson instinctively placed one of the large congratulatory plants on the floor in front of the point. This was the best possible remedy other than cutting off the point, which was not a viable solution.

Remedies for Poison Arrows

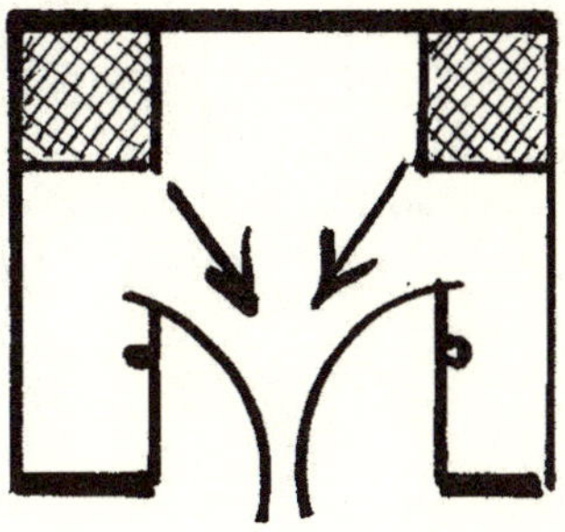

Dressing room poison arrows can detract from the shopping experience.

Take a look around your store and see if you have corners of walls, fixtures, columns or overhanging architectural elements pointing toward:

- Areas where people congregate
- Where customers stop to shop
- Customers in dressing rooms
- Customers or salespeople at the cashwrap
- Customers at the entrance
- Employees in stockrooms or washrooms

If so, you will need to create some remedies to these problems. When you work with remedies, take a moment first to consider what you are doing and your purpose. Don't just toss a plant in front of a sharp corner, walk away and say, "There, that's done!" Stop for a moment and visualize the remedy that would smooth the energy in that area. Focus on the new, positive feeling in that part of the store. Then you can walk away knowing that your intention and the remedy are working together.

Corners on walls or fixtures

Plants are the best remedy for sharp corners that might physically harm a person. In a retail environment, there might not be enough light to keep a plant alive. A silk plant will have the same effect, but make sure to buy the most lifelike plant you can find. Don't skimp! And don't forget to dust the plant regularly.

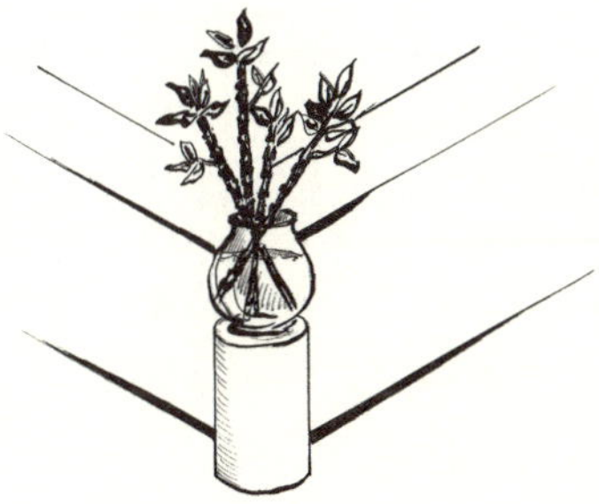

Curve a poison arrow corner with a rounded riser and bamboo.

The ideal plants for a store are green, round-leaved, lush and healthy. If a plant starts to fade or die, don't try to nurture it back to health on the selling floor. It belongs with a caring friend or at home (not in your wealth or relationship

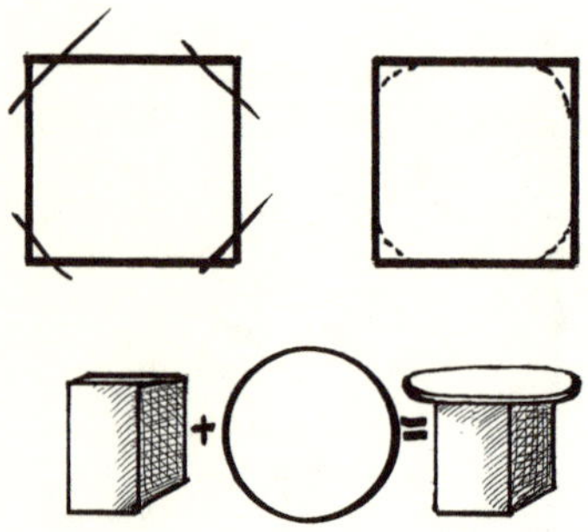

Cut or curve sharp edges or add round tops to angular bases.

areas) until it's come back to health. Avoid plants with sharp, pointy leaves, as well as cactus. They send out their own version of poison arrows.

Another remedy for corners of walls or fixtures is a full, round, cut-glass crystal hung from the ceiling or corner by a red ribbon. This might not work for your store's décor. If crystals are not a workable solution, try a rounded vase with tall, live bamboo stalks or softly shaped branches on the floor in front of the sharp corner. Branches should be placed so that customers' eyes won't get poked while shopping.

Some fixtures can be softened by either cutting the 90-degree top into an octagon, adding a curved top or just turning them slightly out of the main pathway of the customers.

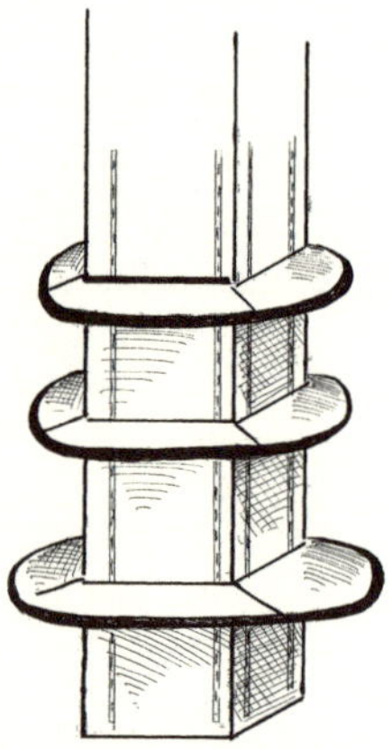

Get the most use out of a column as well as cure its poison arrows.

Columns

If your store has square or rectangular columns, their corners might create poison arrows. Walk around each column and see if you feel uncomfortable in any way. Be aware of your body. Do you tighten up to avoid hitting a corner?

While plants again will work well, there are several other remedies that translate nicely to retail. If your column is within a selling area, consider installing standards on all sides of the column. Have shelves cut with rounded ends so the shelving curves around the column to soften the energy and add space for shelved merchandise. Make sure you add ceiling lights to shine on this new fixture.

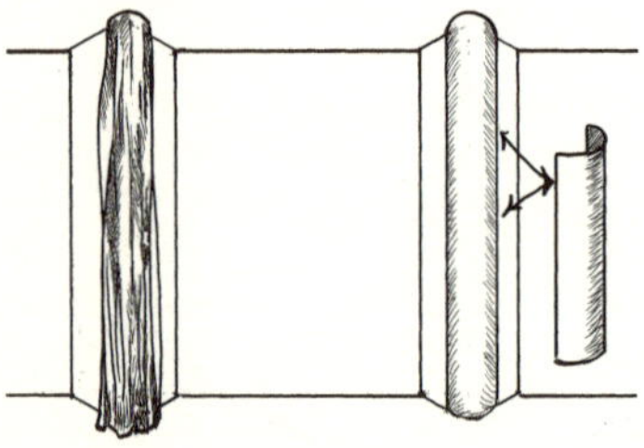

Fabric covering sharp corner and carpet tube cut to cover sharp corner.

Draped fabric can also soften the cutting edges of walls and columns. Of course, the fabric has to work visually with your image and be properly maintained. That means getting it cleaned a minimum of every six months!

Overhanging Architectural Elements and Remedies

While overhanging architectural elements are usually too high to energetically "attack" a customer, they do present their own problems. An exposed overhead beam compresses the energy below, which doesn't matter unless a person is stationed there for any length of time. If that's the case, that person will start feeling ill and end up with a lot of sick days. Most customers don't linger in any part of a store long enough to feel the effects of an overhead beam but when part of the ceiling is lowered in a store, that entire area will feel different. Often ceilings are lowered architecturally to give a store more visual interest and to define spaces. This does work well in stores with ceilings that are more than 12 feet high. However, when the ceilings are lower than 12 feet and then are lowered further to 8 feet by a valance, the energy starts to feel compressed and tight. People might feel a lack of air in lowered areas.

The remedies for this problem are:

- Fans – either on the ceiling or moving air through vents for the HVAC system
- Uplights – lights that shine upward to make the ceiling brighter so it doesn't feel as if it's going to crush a person energetically
- Several faceted, rounded crystals hanging just inches from the ceiling – if they work with your image and décor

Cramped areas might also be called "nooks and crannies." These are usually areas that collect junk and are often poorly lit. A perfect example is the area under a stairwell. In a home, this area is usually walled off and houses suitcases. In a store, it often becomes a storage area. Ceilings slant in these spaces and compress the energy underneath. Lighting combined with great organization is the best remedy for these areas if they aren't walled off from view. If you choose to use one of these areas as storage, keep it neat and clean and make sure the new wall goes from the floor to the angled ceiling.

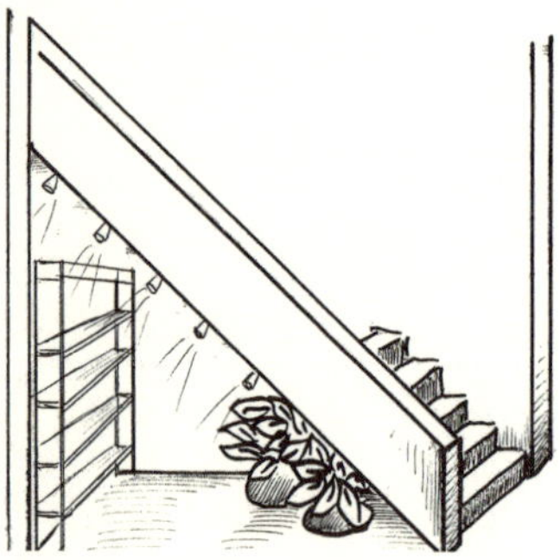
Light up area under stairs — plus use plants to cure stagnant energy.

If you have a lowered, suspended ceiling with fluorescent lights, try to avoid buying parabolic fixtures. Parabolic light fixtures are silver toned and direct the light down to the selling floor. They prevent light from bouncing back onto the ceiling. While having more light on the merchandise is a good thing, the lack of bounced-back ceiling light often makes the ceiling feel lower and dark, creating a cave-like effect. While the selling floor is brighter, the entire store feels dull and dark because the ceiling, the largest visible area, is dark. Replace your parabolic lights with white "egg crate" fixtures or frosted Lucite. Allowing the light to bounce back onto the ceiling will completely change the feeling in your store.

Eliminating Dead Zones

Dead zones are those places in a store where nothing seems to sell. Whatever you put there dies. You don't even want to hang out there in case the bad luck rubs off on you. Every store has dead zones, but the question is why and what can be done to fix them.

Some reasons behind dead zones are:

- Poor lighting
- Overhead fans that are too low
- Compressed energy
- Floor level change
- L-shaped area

- Behind a column
- Poison arrow area
- Lots of angles in ceiling or walls too deep in the store
- Blocked by wall or fixtures

Some remedies are fairly obvious:

- Paint the walls in the dead zone a bright, warm color to add fire energy.
- Add extra light to dark, L-shaped or deep areas.
- Move any fixtures that are blocking the energy from flowing into the area.
- Remove or shorten fans that threaten to "cut off" the heads of customers.
- Remedy poison arrows by adding plants, repositioning fixtures, cutting off sharp edges, adding fabric or crystals.
- If a wall blocks the area, either tear it down, cut it in half or create an aisle that leads directly to the hidden dead zone. Then illuminate it!
- Redirect the traffic flow and the flow of energy by moving floor fixtures to create a new aisle leading into the dead area.
- If there are lots of angles in the walls or ceiling in the dead zone, they will create irritation and arguments. Again, add uplights, some plants and even a few crystals to soften and scatter the negative energy. Don't force people into that area unless absolutely necessary. It might be best for sale items.
- Dead zones are perfect for sale goods. People will cope with all types of bad energy for a good deal!

REVIEW

Chapter Five: Feng Shui and the Selling Floor

1. Whether a store is large or small, the best traffic patterns, according to Feng Shui, **avoid long, straight aisles.**

2. The longer and straighter the aisle, the more quickly energy will flow to the end. In Feng Shui, this has always been considered a negative. Fix this problem with **aisle displays to slow down the traffic.**

3. Consider a **circular aisle plan** to draw customers around your store. A circular plan creates shallow departments, which are proven to sell better.

4. Create a **decompression zone** so your customers have a clear space to decide where they want to go in your store.

5. Start with **low fixtures** in the front of the store and on the aisles, allowing them to become higher the closer they are to the walls. High fixtures in the front of the store and on the aisles block visibility.

6. Make sure **no** fixtures are **blocking** customers from easily walking into your store. Whatever is seen on the first fixture will determine whether or not customers will shop. Lots of varied merchandise on several fixtures will convince them they have many choices.

7. Look for **poison arrows** on the selling floor. They can be created by the angles in fixtures, columns, doors and walls. People will feel uncomfortable standing in their pathways.

8. Plants or rounded fixtures are the best **remedies for poison arrows.** Fabric can also be a cure but must work with your décor to be effective.

9. **Overhanging architectural** structures compress the energy below them. This can lead to chronic illness. Aiming lights upward to light up the surface will alleviate the problem.

10. **Dead zones** in your store are the areas where nothing seems to sell. Some basic remedies include: better lighting; painting with a bright, warm color; removing blocking walls or fixtures; redirecting the traffic flow by creating a new aisle; remedying any poison arrows; reinstalling fans and lights so they are higher. If needed, and if all else fails, make the dead zone into the clearance area.

Selling Floor Quiz

This first exercise takes some time, but the results are worth the time spent.

1. Keep an eye on your front door for a minimum of one day but preferably two – one weekday and one Saturday. On a notepad, keep track of which direction people turn as they walk into your store. If possible, note their progress throughout the store. If your store is wonderfully busy, do the best you can to keep track.

Give this exercise to others on the staff so customer movement is recorded for at least seven days total. You might want to create a chart to make it easier:

Left	Right	Straight	Slight Left	Slight Right	Circled Store	Zig-Zagged Store	Left Store	Other

Once you recognize customer movement, you can determine how to improve the traffic flow.

2. Look for poison arrows in your store. Make a list of all you find and decide if you want to soften them. If so, determine what cure or remedy will work best for each situation.

Poison Arrow
Cure/Remedy

3. Walk outside your store, turn around and start to walk back in and stop:

- What is the first thing you see?

____

____

- Does the store feel dark or light?

____

____

- Do you know what is sold in the store based on what you see first? __________________

- Is there a clear aisle pathway?

____

____

- Do you feel restricted by any fixtures that are too tall?

____

4. As you walk down an aisle...

- Do any fixtures prevent you from moving easily through the store?

  List these fixtures:

  1.
  2.
  3.
  4.
  5.

5. List five things you can do right now to make it easier for customers to "read" and walk through your store.

1.

____
____
____
____
____
____

2.

____
____
____
____
____
____

3.

4.

5.

6

Color and Your Store

Basics of Color

Color evokes emotional, physical and psychic sensations. Colors heal, irritate, soothe or create feelings of joy and contentment. Colors make us feel warm, cold, anxious or calm. Using color with knowledge and intent helps you paint and decorate your store intelligently to allow you to achieve your desired effect.

Colors have symbolism in Chinese Feng Shui just as they do in Western color psychology. Color symbolism very often transcends cultural differences. Red has the same effect in every culture as do yellow, blue, green and so on. There are many color theories, but it all comes down to you. It's important that you work with colors you enjoy – not just ones you feel you "should" use because some book tells you they're correct for a certain section.

Each area of the Bagua chart is represented by a different color. This can be a problem when you're trying to achieve a cohesive look in your store. If you want to work with traditional Feng Shui colors in each ninth of your store, you will end up with a fairly unattractive and chopped-up looking store. A better way to use "proper" Feng Shui colors is to bring them into their ideal areas through accessories and props.

In retail environments, color can be a powerful thing:
Bright colors heighten energy – good for younger customers or customers who perceive themselves to be young.
Dark colors slow down energy – good for areas where you want people to feel comfortable and take their time shopping (for example, in furniture stores).
Pastel colors soften energy – good for harsh areas such as inner cities, areas with strong weather extremes or brightly colored malls.
Reds, golds and purples attract energy and sales – good for the wealth and fame sections of your store.
White, beiges and tans neutralize energy – good for stores with lots of bright merchandise but with an older customer base.
Oranges and green-blues heighten creativity – good for stores with trendsetting or handcrafted merchandise.
Purples, violets and white strengthen spirituality – good for stores dealing with plants and nature, new-age products or religious items.

Colors from the sun – oranges, reds, pinks, yellows and yellow-greens – warm people and are excellent for cold climates in the winter.

Colors from the sky and sea – greens, blues and lavenders – cool people off and are excellent in warm climates as focal wall colors.

Softer pinks, toned-down reds and oranges – unlike their brighter tones, these colors just make people feel warm and friendly.

Hot pinks, reds, black and soft oranges suggest sexuality – great for stores that sell products such as lingerie, essential oils and adult toys.

Browns, tans, taupes, beiges and deeper reds ground and inspire trust and bring us down to earth – perfect for home products, books and handcrafted items. (For electronics, use deeper reds and browns.)

Burgundy, red, royal blue, gold and black are the power colors – good for high-priced merchandise but most effective when used in smaller amounts. In large amounts, they are overwhelming.

Color and the Elements of Nature

When selecting colors for your store, keep in mind how colors can evoke the various elements of nature:

Wood = green tones – encourages expansion, growth, healing, intuition. Found in wood fixturing, columns and vertical shapes, plants/flowers (real or silk), cotton or rayon fabrics, art that represents the outdoors, paper, paneling and wood flooring.

Fire = reds, yellows and oranges – enhances fame, emotions, action. Found in triangles, pyramids and cone shapes, lighting – all types – any animal products such as suede, fur, feathers, wool, silk and leather, animals, art showing light sources (sun, fire, etc.).

Metal = white, silver, chrome, gold and bronze – enhances mental sharpness.
Too much = rigidity, stubbornness, lack of teamwork.
Too little = indecisiveness, procrastination and confusion.
Found in all metals, metal fixtures, cement, rocks, stones (for example, marble, granite), crystals, circular, oval and arched shapes and architectural elements.
Earth = all shades of brown and yellow from deep golds to pale tones – strengthens stability, practicality, strength, grounding.
Too much = heavy, serious, closed in, binding.
Too little = instability, clutter, chaos.
Found in brick, clay tiles, ceramic and earthenware pieces, square and rectangular shapes, and art showing earthy landscapes.
Water = blues, black, dark colors – encourages spirituality, inspiration, relaxation, flexibility.
Too much = promotes spaciness and hurts productivity.
Too little = develops stress, anxiety, pettiness, sarcasm and rivalry.
Found in water features of all types, reflective surfaces such as glass and mirrors, freeform, flowing, asymmetrical shapes and flowing fabrics.

Energy Color Chart*

Effects on Moods and Energy	*Colors*
Lifts energy	yellows, reds, turquoise, bright colors
Slows down energy	browns, rusts, all dark colors
Softens energy	light pinks and greens, corals, pastels

Draws energy	reds, golds, rich purples
Neutralizes energy	white, beiges, tans
Enhances creativity	oranges, turquoise, teals, vibrant blues
Enhances spirituality	purples, violets, white
Warming colors	reds, oranges, yellows, yellow-green
Cooling colors	blues, blue-green, lavender
Romantic colors	pinks, reds, oranges, warm greens
Sexual colors	reds, black, oranges, hot pink
Grounding colors	reds, browns, tans, beiges
Power colors	golds, black, burgundy, reds, royal blue
Soothing colors	greens, blues, peach

Painting Your Walls: What Each Color Means

Before you decide on a color, it's important to understand what each color brings to the table.

---

* Thanks to:

Nancy SantoPietro, author of *Feng Shui: Harmony by Design*, Berkley Publishing Group, 1996.

Neutrals: When you paint your store walls in neutral colors such as taupe, tans or grays, you create a quieter energy in the store. If you have a lot of brightly colored merchandise, these neutrals can work well. If your merchandise is also subdued in color, the overall effect of your store will be quiet and somewhat dull – not fabulous for sales.

White: White is not considered a neutral. In essence it repels energy just as it repels sunlight. When energy is repelled, it has to go somewhere – usually bouncing around the store. Too much white might cause anxiety. It is best used as an accent to break up other colors. White combined with other colors creates a balance of light and dark (or darker than white) plus a balance of energy in your store. White is a great ceiling color because it bounces light back to the selling floor and will keep the wall colors from "bleeding" into the ceiling. White denotes purity, cleanliness, freshness and honesty. Bright white is not great in cold climates or any spaces where you want people to interact in a friendly manner. It discourages warmth both in temperature and personalities.

Red: Representing the fire element, red is considered to be the luckiest color of all. It has Yang energy – male life force power. In small amounts, nothing sells like red. Although it is an excellent small accent color, too much bright red can be annoying and irritating. It's been said that five minutes in a red room feels like 25 minutes. Think Macy's at Christmas. Time just drags because the red throws off so much energy that some people start feeling drained. It also throws heat. If your store is in a warm climate, too much red will drive air-conditioning costs sky high as your customers and staff complain about the heat. If you live in a cold climate and want to warm up, wear red.

Bright "Chinese Red" is best used in small amounts in decorative accessories such as flowers, vases, egg shapes or bowls. Toned-down reds "sell" just as well but are less irritating. Toned-down reds include burgundy, cranberry, pink shades, dark reds with blue added or muted reds with green added to dull the brightness.

Pink: Especially when using lighter shades including bubble-gum pink, this color opens the heart while reducing stress and anxiety. Pink shades are great for high-strung people of any age. Soft pink calms people down and creates a friendly environment.

Purple: Considered a very lucky color, purple welcomes money into your store when combined with chrome or silver. Because "red purples" have a religious connotation, it makes sense to use blue-toned purples unless your store sells religious-oriented merchandise. Blue-toned purples are also found in shades of lavender.

It is said that shoplifting is reduced in a store with lots of purple. The author's theory is that shoplifters wait 11 seconds, say a quick prayer that they aren't caught, and steal just as much.

Yellow: Yellow is as lucky as red and purple. It is considered to bring good fortune to a space and used to be the Imperial color of old China. It represents moving forward, fame, luck and fortune.

Yellow is the first color that is seen by the retina of the eye. It strengthens mental activity and says "stop and think." A wonderful accent color, it's best found in the center of your store. Too much yellow will pull the eye all over the place, making it difficult to focus on any one area. Use yellow sparingly where you want focal points to pop. Because it reflects on skin tones, making them sallow, use it away from dressing rooms and mirrors.

You can use yellow in signage, props, flower bouquets, décor items or an area rug. Another option is to place yellow and earth-toned merchandise in the center of your store – your center of balance and energy.

Orange: Although it's one of the least personally favorite colors in the world, orange is most favored by artists and trendsetters. Orange is the combination of red and yellow. Red is life force energy and blood, while yellow represents the sun. Orange, the color of creativity, also represents affordability in today's culture. Orange is a warm, friendly color that encourages people to interact more – making it great for sections of your store that require conversations with customers. Orange does not encourage focused concentration or peacefulness. It can be used to pep up a wall and to give fresh life and energy to a section of a store. Toning orange down into terra cotta will achieve the dual effects of adding energy and friendliness to your store.

Green: Considered the color of wood energy, green symbolizes growth, expansion, nature and healing. Green encourages action but is not an "action" color like red, yellow or orange. The opposite of red, green relaxes people and encourages them to stay longer in a store. It's been found that 20 minutes in a green room feels like only five minutes have passed. Green heals the heart and calms the mind. Soft, muted shades of green are restful and sophisticated.

Blue: Blue is the color of communication, adventure and exploration. Medium-blue shades are reputed to be men's most favorite colors. Blue is also, in large amounts, somewhat depressing. There is no heart energy associated with blue and to have good sales, you need for people's hearts to be touched.

Sky or pale blue creates the feeling of expansion that is great for small spaces or low ceilings. It must be modified with a warm color to keep the store energized. For a small space, consider a pale-blue ceiling with soft yellow walls to add warmth, energy and luck.

Dark blue is very serious and official. It says authority and is rarely used to good effect in a retail store.

Black: This non-color absorbs all colors and reflects nothing back. It's best used in small amounts to define an area or as an accent on fixtures. Too much black can be depressing and cause customers and staff to feel exhausted and overwhelmed. Black ceilings absorb light and might create a cave-like feel. You will need to almost triple your lighting to adequately light your merchandise if you have a black ceiling.

A black ceiling can be softened with the use of a white ceiling grid with inset lights but no ceiling tiles. In this way, the black will achieve some clarity and structure. If you have a black ceiling in your store and your fixtures are shelves, try to keep the shelving color as light as possible to reflect light back on your merchandise.

REVIEW

Chapter Six: Color and Your Store

1. Colors have a psychological, emotional, physical and psychic impact on all people. Understanding their **meanings and power** will help you decide what colors to paint your store.

2. Each area of the **Bagua chart** is represented by a different color. A great way to use "proper" Feng Shui colors is to bring them into their ideal areas through accessories and props.

3. **Bright colors** heighten energy.
Dark colors slow down energy.
Pastel colors soften energy.

Reds, golds and purples attract energy and sales.
White, beiges and tans neutralize energy.
Oranges and green-blues heighten creativity.
Purples, violets and white strengthen spirituality.

4. **Wood** = green tones – encourages expansion, growth, healing and intuition.
Fire = reds, yellows and oranges – enhances fame, emotions and action.
Metal = white, silver, chrome, gold and bronze – enhances mental sharpness.
Earth = all shades of brown and yellow from deep golds to pale tones – strengthens stability, practicality, strength and grounding.
Water = blues, black, dark colors – encourages spirituality, inspiration, relaxation and flexibility.

5. **Neutrals:** If you have a lot of brightly colored merchandise, neutral tones can work well.

6. **White:** This is not a neutral. White is an excellent ceiling color and accent color. Pure white walls will bounce energy around the store. If your walls are broken up by lots of merchandise and fixtures, white walls will work. But too much white will cause anxiety.

7. **Red:** Considered to be the luckiest color of all, red represents the fire element. Red has Yang energy – male life force power. In small amounts, nothing sells like red.

8. **Purple:** A very lucky color, purple, when combined with chrome or silver, welcomes money into your store.

9. **Yellow:** Like red and purple, yellow is a lucky color that represents moving forward, fame, luck and fortune.

10. **Black:** A non-color, black absorbs all colors and reflects nothing back. You will need to almost triple your lighting to adequately light your merchandise if you have a black ceiling.

References:
Feng Shui: Harmony by Design by Nancy SantoPietro, Berkley Publishing Group, 1996
The Feng Shui Kit by Man Et Al Ho Kwok, Charles E. Tuttle Co., Inc., 1995
The Western Guide to Feng Shui: Room by Room by Terah Kathryn Collins, Hay House, 1999
Feng Shui: The Book of Cures by Nancilee Wydra, McGraw-Hill, 1996
Feng Shui Made Easy by William Spear, HarperCollins, 1995

7

Your Walls and Feng Shui

Just as Feng Shui is the understanding of the connection between all things, your walls are the connection and stability of your store and as such require thought and care. The walls of your store are broken into three parallel areas. From the floor to about 3 feet up is considered the past. From 3 to 6½ feet is the present. And 6½ feet to the ceiling is the future.

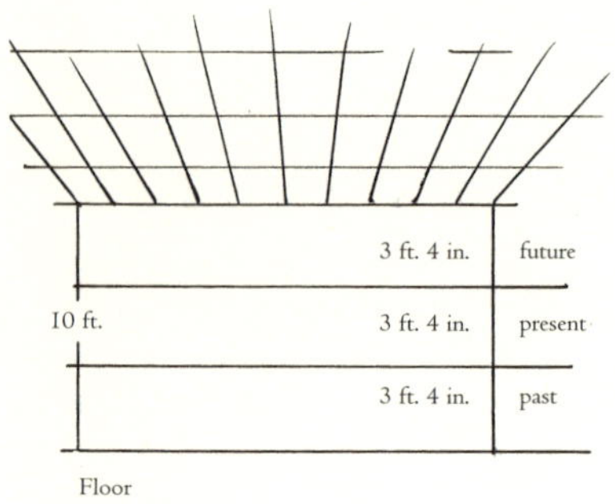

Basic retail logic agrees with this ancient concept. Generally, people don't like to bend, so the present – between 3 and 6½ feet from the floor – is the main selling area. Below is where you put duplicates or broken assortments, and above 6½ feet is unreachable for many, so it becomes an excellent area for display.

Walls and Flow

Whenever possible, to get the best flow in your store, angle your walls so the energy flows smoothly around your store's perimeter. Ninety-degree angles trap energy and are difficult to fixture effectively. When you angle the corners, you won't lose much hanging or shelving space, plus you'll pick up extra, new and powerful focal areas. Make sure there are incandescent spotlights trained on these prime focal areas.

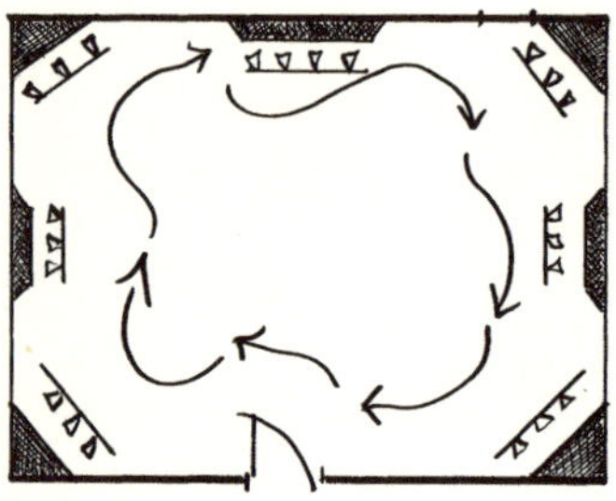

Angled walls create better energy flow.

Walls and the Elements

While textured walls are always positive in store design, there are some textures that are better than others, according to the principles of Feng Shui. Each texture suggests an element.

Water = introspection and intuition. For a retailer, it's easiest to represent the water element through the use of glass. Your glass shelves are the water element in your store and add balance to the woods and metals. Any fabric or material that flows or changes shape suggests water. Fabric with undulating lines may also represent water on a wall but in retail, using strongly patterned fabric behind merchandise rarely works well. Solid-color flowing fabric will work better than prints if the fabric flows freely and doesn't look skimpy.

Beware of dust and dirt buildup on the bottom of the fabric if it drapes luxuriously on the floor. Make sure your fabric is easy to take down, clean and reinstall, otherwise it will forever look dirty and, by association, so will your merchandise.

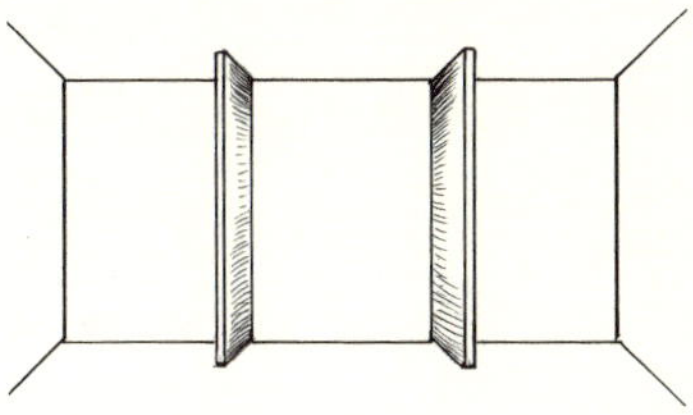

Wall breaks.

Wood = growth. While wood-covered walls are obviously the wood element, any dimensional or vertical architectural component will also represent growth. Wood encourages creativity and expansion. Too much wood can be overwhelming, while too little can create sluggish, slow growth and a lack of energy.

Vertical wall breaks suggest trees. If you don't want to have wood on your walls, the vertical elements will act as wood. From a retailer's point of view, wall breaks are an excellent way to create interesting walls and allow you to separate classifications, categories and colors.

Varied wall statements.

Creating a different visual statement every 3 to 5 feet between structural wall breaks is a great way to make your store more interesting and appealing while adding to its success. All plants or plant-based fabrics represent the wood element, as does artwork showing landscapes, gardens, flowers and trees.

Fire = energy starter. The fire element activates interactions between people and is vital to achieving good sales in a store. It is represented by triangles – the best shape for many displays.

On a wall, the fire element can be represented by displays on shelves with some red-toned accents; a chevron pattern on the wall; anything from animals (including leather, feathers, bones and wool); art showing suns, fire, people or animals; and lights (including spotlights shining on the walls or lighted lamps on shelves).

Triangle display.

Too much fire can cause irritation, impatience and even fights. Remember: fire is represented by red! Too little fire can feel cold, dull and unemotional. Shopping is an emotional experience, so it's vital to add fire elements to strengthen the energy of your store.

Earth = strong, practical and stable. Square or rectangular shapes represent this element. They hold things up and keep them safe. Bricks, tiles, ceramics, cement, earth tones and earthenware all make us feel protected and unified. Squares create boundaries that allow us to stay centered within the store and ourselves.

On your store walls, you can create a firm, good feeling with the use of terra cotta, bricks, adobe, framed landscapes as well as the rectangles and squares created by shelving, rods and wall breaks. Of course, stucco can be either great or awful. Whether it's good Feng Shui depends upon how it's applied.

Sharp points are negative, while smoothed-out swirls are positive. Sharp edges create tension and can harm flesh and fragile merchandise. Smoothed, curved swirls suggest positive things such as the earth (and the metal element) as well as soft, swelling hills. Too many earth elements can start feeling overwhelming and heavy while too little can feel unstable, encouraging disorganization and clutter.

Metal = strengthens the mind. Using metal laminates or faux metal directly on your walls will create an intensely strong metal element in your store. Too much metal might create stubbornness combined with poor teamwork – awful for a retail store. Not enough metal can aid in indecisiveness, procrastination and confusion – not terrific for sales! It makes sense to find a good balance of metals in your store. Luckily, any type of curved architectural elements or curved fixtures, including round tables, cabinets, door handles and round mirrors, represents the metal element.

Metals are found in most fixtures, especially in and on the walls. Inside the walls are metal studs and wiring, while standards and brackets are most often metal. Steel gray, gold, copper, brass and silver paint remind us of different metals. Avoid metal walls without the softening elements of wood, water (glass/fabric) and earth (tiles/square shapes/earth tones).

Elements and Wall Texture

Don't overdo any one look or material. Strive for balance. Too much wood without the balancing elements of water (glass), fire (triangles and lights), earth (bricks, square shapes) and metal (rounded shapes, stones, white/pastels) can feel dull and too heavy. Too much metal feels cold, unyielding and rigid. Too much water (glass) will feel ungrounded, while too much fire (reds, triangles) can create tension, anxiety and arguments. If the idea of an all (pick one) metal, glass, cement, tile, red-toned, wood store appeals to you, make sure your merchandise and displays fill in and balance the rest of the elements.

Walls and Fixturing

Interior walls are the equivalent to the windows of your store. Each wall tells customers exactly who your store is and what you believe in. Your wall fixtures should reflect your image and your merchandise. Any conflict of image is confusing to your customers. For example, you don't want to see cheap grid mixed with handcrafted glassware. Nor does a carved, inlaid wood fixture work for small appliances. Consistency of image begins with store design and fixturing.

There are many different types and styles of wall fixtures. Each has its own energy as well as practical use and image.

Standards and brackets: You can merchandise almost anything on basic standards and brackets. They can be elegant, inset and invisible, basic chrome, colorful, powder coated, raw metal or wood. Standards and brackets create a strong

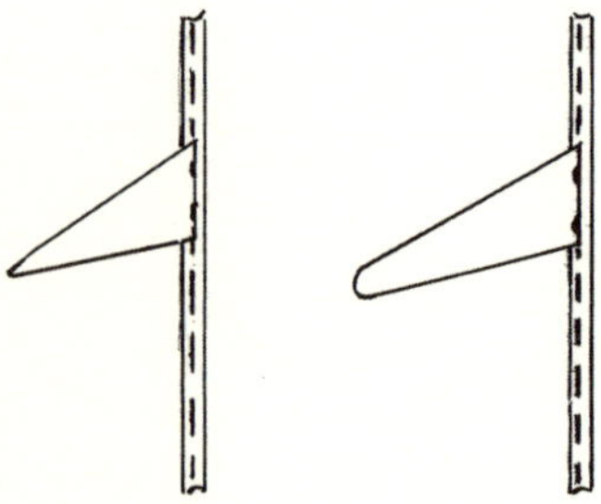

Pointed bracket (left) and rounded bracket (right).

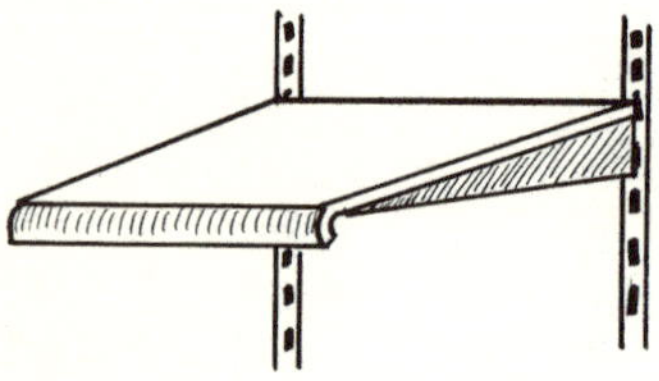

"Faux" dimensional shelf with lip covering brackets.

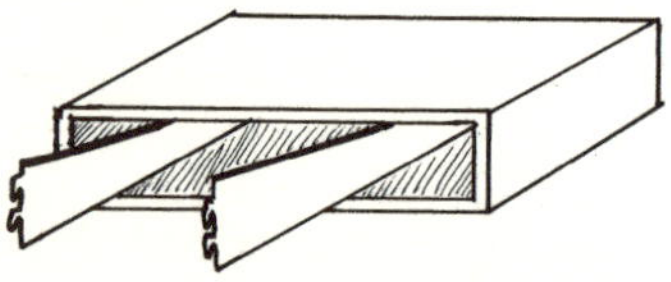

Dimensional box covering brackets.

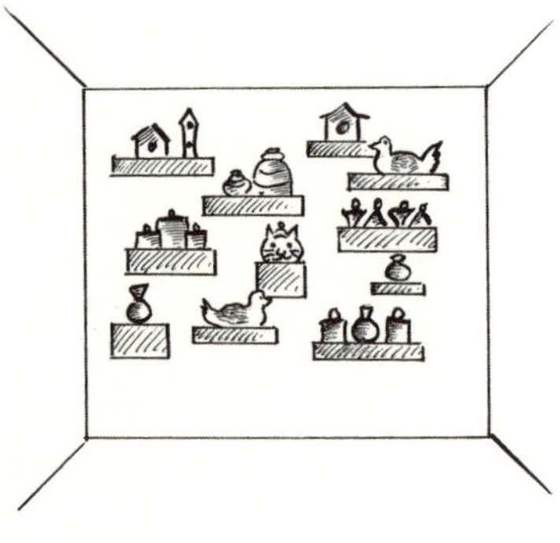

Dimensional shelves.

vertical and horizontal feel to a store. The vertical is the standard and the horizontal is in the perpendicular bracket that runs parallel to the floor. The brackets can be a positive element if they have rounded ends. If their ends are pointy and sharp, they become negative as they feel energetically like a knife pointed at the body of the shopper. Pointy brackets are considered to be "poison arrows."

An excellent way to alleviate any poison arrows created by wall brackets is to buy dimensional shelving that hides the bracket in one of two ways. It can be a hollow shelf that slips over the bracket, or it can be a flat shelf with a wide lip that hides the face of the bracket from view. Either solution is a good Feng Shui remedy and improves the overall look of your walls with more dimensional and substantial shelves.

Standards and brackets are also used for hanging clothing. Once again, avoid sharp brackets and buy the type that holds metal tubing – usually slightly curved and less threatening energetically. The basic rule of walls and Feng Shui is to avoid poison arrows. Don't have sharp things sticking out from your walls!

Slatwall: Unless they are completely covered by merchandise, the powerful horizontal lines of slatwall are very visually distracting and annoying. Slatwall was originally designed to display shoes – especially athletic sneakers. Lots of small shelves holding lightweight objects are perfect for slatwall. Large shelves holding heavy items or long hang bars for clothing are a poor use of this material.

Slatwall is not designed to hold very heavy merchandise and while it holds lots of small items perfectly, it is not a viable or pleasing decorative element. In large amounts, it can tire the eyes by forcing them to follow long, parallel lines. It is most effectively used in smaller areas and looks best when framed out to create an attractive wall break. Consider buying unfinished slatwall so you can paint and repaint, as your store requires change.

Grid: Similar to slatwall, grid sets up a strong visual pattern that can overwhelm your product. Because the earth element is represented by squares and rectangles, metal grid has qualities of both the earth and metal elements. It constricts the overall feeling of a store with its strong graphic lines. Grid is best used when it's covered completely by merchandise. Whatever is displayed on grid immediately loses its perceived value and appears inexpensive. Use it sparingly – if at all. The best use for grid is when it's hung from the ceiling, parallel to the floor and ceiling in a window or over display tables. Hanging grids make display easy and more flexible.

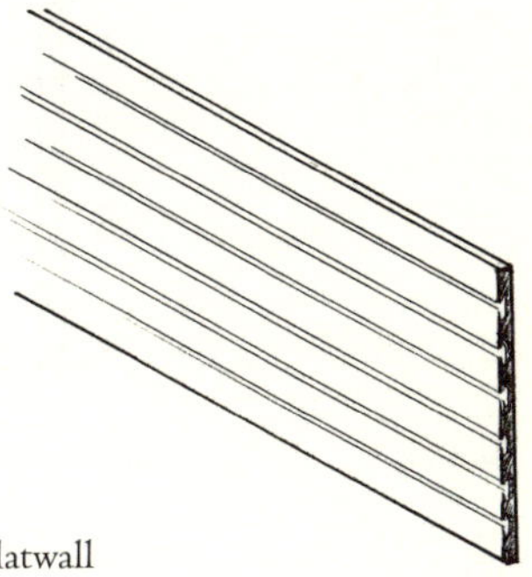

Slatwall

Pegboard: This "old-fashioned" material is making a comeback as a gentler form of slatwall and grid. The hanging fixtures for pegboard are much less attractive and although its "old hardware store" history makes it seem dated, it can take on a new life with a bright-colored paint or frame. Also used to sell many small items, pegboard should be as fully merchandised as possible as the holes are a visual distraction. Pegboard is the wood element and defines its space.

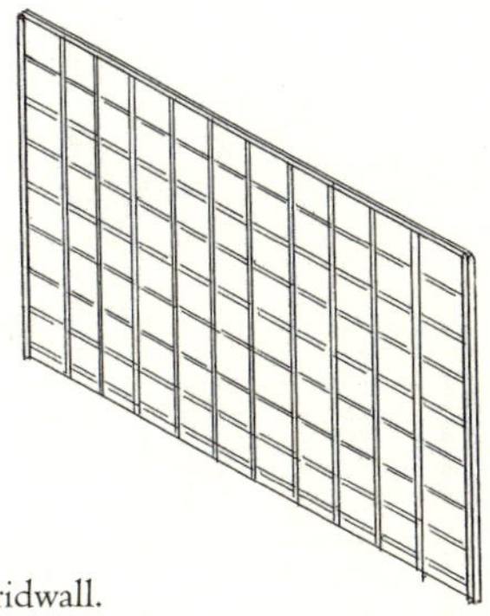

Gridwall.

Pucks: Pucks are a newer form of slatwall, grid and pegboard. The puck system uses larger holes that are set further apart to hold shelves, rods, face-outs or individual pieces of merchandise. Perfect for hanging or shelving merchandising, the puck system works on glass, wood or metal, and the pucks can either match the material they are on or be in a contrasting color.

What makes pucks interesting and exciting are their freshness plus the variety of material combinations available. One store in New York City used frosted-glass panels against its walls with white pucks holding up brushed silver metal

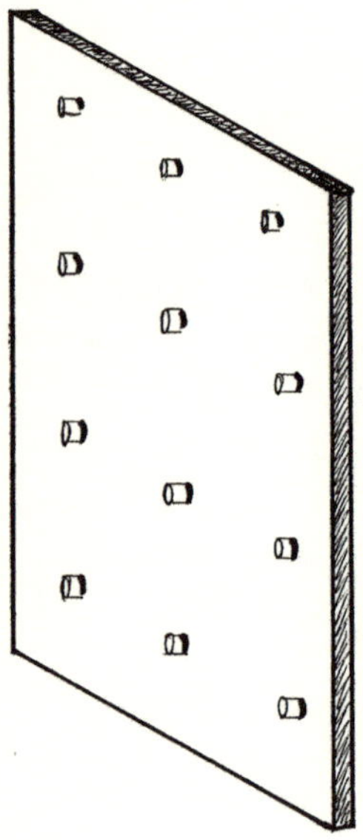

Puck wall.

hang rods. The elements were balanced on the wall with the use of decorative square paintings and red clothing.

Here are some fixturing elements and what they represent in Feng Shui:

Glass Panels = Water
Wood Hangers = Wood
Square Pictures = Earth
Metal Pucks = Metal
Red Clothing = Fire

Cable Systems: These interesting hanging and shelving systems are made of wire, metal and – most often – glass. Because this mix can be cold and unforgiving, it works best against textured walls either of stucco, wood or fabric. In other words, it needs another element to balance the metal and water.

Balance is vital in all store design. Customers feel more comfortable when there is a balance of soft and hard surfaces. A display with all glass and metal feels too cold. But adding wood, fire and earth completes the wall and makes it more appealing and accessible.

Wall Cubes: These earth element fixtures are like a three-dimensional grid. Visually, they work best when completely filled. If you find yourself low on stock, have some filler prop available for your empty cubes. An empty cube is a visual red flag to your customers that says you are "sold down" and whatever remains is a left-over, picked-over and rejected piece. Even a teddy bear is preferable to an empty square space.

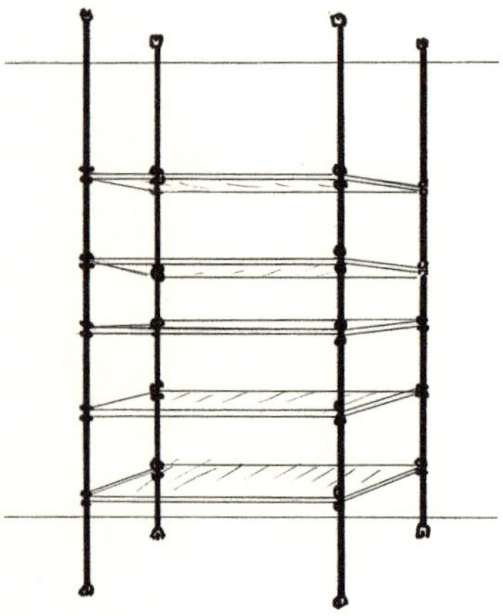

Cable system

Freestanding Shelving, Armoires and Built-in Areas: Each of these display fixtures creates a rectangle grounding the wall with the earth element. They are most often made of wood with metal handles, hooks, rods and shelf clips. Glass shelves add the water element. Each of these units acts as a wall break and makes a wall more interesting, while bringing in a balance of elements. On the other hand, there is little flow created by these types of fixtures because each section exists entirely on its own. In order to visually connect these separate fixtures from a distance, you can:

1. Create similar or coordinated boutique merchandise statements on the top shelves.

2. Place related props in each area to tie them in visually.

3. Connect through color.

You do this because your store is an entity and each section, while separate and telling its own story, is part of the whole, and that entity needs to be addressed and honored.

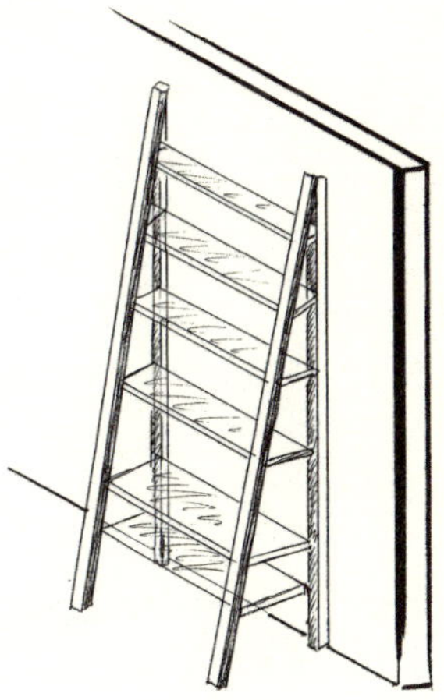

Leaning wood wall fixture

Angled/Leaning Shelves: Some newer shelving units lean against a wall rather than the shelves having all the same depth. The positive aspect of leaning or angled shelves is that they lead the energy of your store and merchandise up from the past to the future with a strong visually angled line. Their only negative is that if they are too strongly angled, it might be difficult for shorter people to reach the higher shelves. If that's the case in your store, use those higher shelves for displays rather than stock.

Lighting Your Walls

Good lighting is vital to the sales health of your store. If people can't see it, they can't buy it! Trying to save money by scrimping on lights will come back to haunt you. That said, you could save money by using fluorescent wall washers combined with incandescent spot and floodlights.

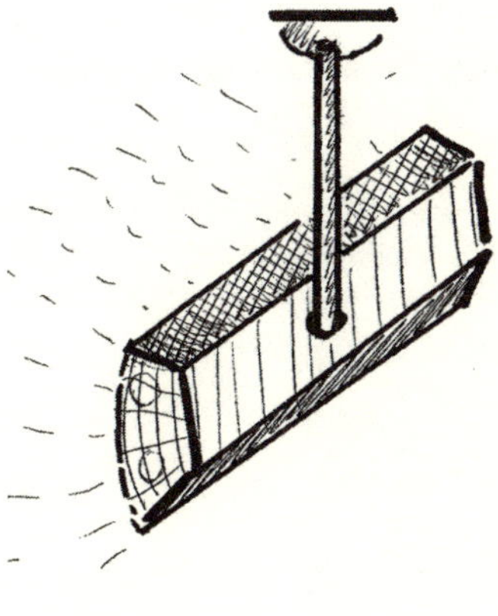

Fluorescent wall washer

Fluorescent wall washers will bathe a wall with general illumination. Although this light will strengthen the brightness of an area, the wall will still need incandescent spots, floods or halogen lights to make the merchandise "pop." It will just need fewer spotlights when combined with the wall washers. While fluorescent wall washers cost more upfront, they generally pay for themselves with lower electricity costs within one and a half to two years. If you have a five- to 10-year lease, you will save substantially by using wall washers. A good plus is that you can take them with you if you relocate.

Lights add energy to your store. When lights are too low or dim, the entire space feels closed in and oppressive. A cave-like effect can turn off customers unwilling to negotiate a new place without benefit of light.

Interesting fact: Fluorescent light bulbs start to dim the day they are installed. They dim slowly so you won't notice the decreased light on a day-to-day basis. However, your customers, who only come in from time to time, will be aware of the store's dimness. When you buy fluorescent bulbs, buy enough to fully change out your ceiling twice. When the first bulb dies, you know it's time to replace all the bulbs at once. The rest will go soon and they are throwing considerably less light than when they were installed.

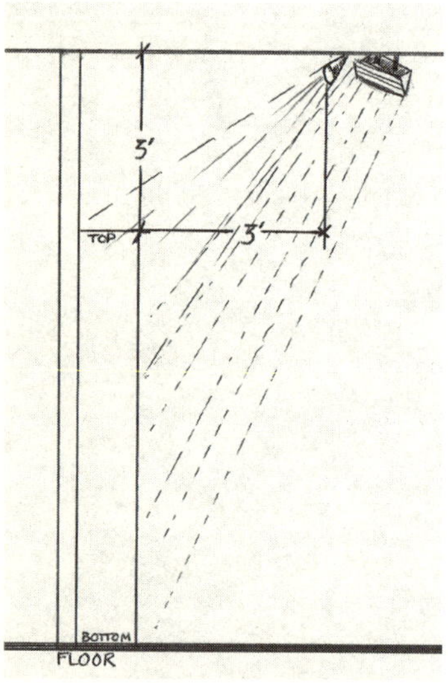

Mount track lights and wall washers 3 feet out from the fixture face and 3 feet from the top of the fixture.

For the greatest lighting advantage to all concerned, consider installing full-spectrum lights. They cost more but are worth every penny. They imitate the sun, and all colors of the spectrum pop under this light. In terms of Feng Shui and good logic, full-spectrum lights make sense.

Use commercial-grade lights only. If you can buy lighting at a hardware store, it is most likely for the home market and will burn out quickly with the high demand of retail stores. Speak to a lighting consultant, a lighting manufacturer's representative or to a sales associate in a specialized lighting store. Don't go it alone!

A quick lighting rule: Measure 3 feet from the top/front of your fixtures straight out into the store. Now, measure approximately 3 feet up from that point, and that's the ideal place for your spots, floods or fluorescents.

Walls and Merchandising

The art of placement is a common description of Feng Shui. How merchandise is placed on a wall is vital to the selling success of the store. In Feng Shui, clutter is a killer. The more simple, organized and clean your walls, the better the energy in your store. A lack of visual organization on a wall makes the clutter more important than individual pieces of merchandise.

Each wall section can tell a separate story as long as the stories all work together to form a cohesive "story book." Wall breaks can give you the perfect way to separate and show a "by use" story, a color story, a vendor story and a classification story.

By Use: Refers to items that are used together. Example: A salad wall could feature bowls, lettuce crispers, lettuce driers, graters, utensils, vegetable cleaners, chopping knives and blocks.

By Color: Showcases merchandise by color. While there is still a need to keep "use" in mind, you can pull together all items of a color group. Example: Create a display using accessories in various shades of pink: scarves, necklaces, bags, shoes, socks/hosiery, sweaters, undergarments, blouses and bottoms. Of course if you are selling Stihl chainsaws, the company pulls the orange color together for you and your wall will look coordinated thanks to their products and graphics.

By Vendor: Groups products that are obviously from one vendor (such as Krups, Stihl, Jones of New York or Gold Toe).

You will still need to coordinate sub-groups within this larger group. Use color stories to coordinate an overall vendor wall.

By Classification: Displays one type of product on one wall, such as cutlery, motor oils, cutting instruments, hosiery, jewelry, etc. This type of display brings up sub-classifications. For example, an all-jewelry wall breaks down to silver, gold, costume, handmade, custom, diamonds and other precious stones. By adding wall breaks to your walls, you allow these different groups to have their own identities and tell their individual stories.

If you don't have physical wall breaks on your walls, you can create a visual break by leaving space between stories. While you lose 4 to 6 inches of valuable hanging space, you gain immeasurably with visual clarity.

Remember to display in the future, mass out merchandise in the present, and put duplicates or sale items below 3 feet in the past.

REVIEW

Chapter Seven: Your Walls and Feng Shui

1. The **walls** of your store are broken into three parallel areas. From the floor to about 3 feet up is considered the past. From 3 to 6½ feet is the present, and 6½ feet to the ceiling is the future.

2. **90-degree angles** trap energy and are difficult to fixture effectively. When you angle the corners, you won't lose much hanging or shelving space, plus you'll pick up extra, new and powerful focal areas.

3. Too much **wood** in a store can be overwhelming, while too little can create sluggish, slow growth and a lack of energy.

4. **Water** represents introspection and inspiration. The water element can be found in glass or any undulating lines. Moving water indicates social networking.

5. **Fire** is an energy starter. It activates interactions between people and is vital to achieving good sales in a store. It's represented by triangles – the best shape for many displays.

6. **Earth** is represented by square or rectangular shapes. Earth elements are strong, practical and stable. They hold things up and keep them safe.

7. **Metal** strengthens the mind. Using metal laminates or faux metal directly on your walls will create an intensely strong metal element to your store. Too much metal might create stubbornness combined with poor teamwork.

8. **Brackets** can be a positive element if they have rounded ends. If their ends are pointy and sharp they become negative, as they feel energetically like a knife pointed at the body of the shopper. Pointy brackets are considered to be "poison arrows."

9. An excellent way to alleviate any **poison arrows** created by wall brackets is to buy dimensional shelving that hides the brackets.

10. Unless they are completely covered by merchandise, the powerful horizontal lines or squares of **slatwall** and **grid wall** are very visually distracting and annoying.

11. **Balance** is vital in all store design. Customers feel more comfortable when there is a balance of soft and hard surfaces. All glass and metal feels too cold. Adding wood, fire and earth completes the wall and makes it more appealing and accessible.

Wall Audit

Pretend you are a customer and walk into your store for the first time.

1. Note which walls you see first, second, third and fourth.

    1.
    2.
    3
    4.

2 What sections of each of these walls are visible?

    1.
    2.
    3.
    4.

3. Walk through your store and notice what the walls are saying to you. If they are "telling a story," you've done a good job. If they are a mish-mash of items with no logical adjacencies, you've confused your customers.

The story is:

1.
2.
3.
4.

4. Look at each wall and list the elements you find:

	water	earth	fire	metal	wood
1.					
2.					
3.					
4.					
5.					
6.					

Are the elements on each wall balanced? Can you add merchandise to help achieve balance?

If you don't think you can be objective, ask your best customers, friends and family to do this visual audit for you.

8

Non-Selling Spaces and Feng Shui

In Feng Shui, your non-selling spaces are as important as the selling floor. The energy generated by unseen areas influences all aspects of your store's success. Your non-selling spaces include your office, stockroom, bathrooms and hallways, as well as storage space above or below your selling floor. Energy flow has been discussed throughout this book, and it's equally vital that the energy be clear and unblocked in all areas of your leased space.

The Office

It's your sanctuary, your refuge from crazed, full moon customers trying to return 10-year-old socks because they are "worn out." Your office is the place where you regroup, think, order, reorder, pay bills and accomplish about a thousand other tasks. Your office is the heart of your store. It should make you feel refreshed, reenergized, alert and calm. If you don't feel any of these things, it's time to rethink the space.

First, do you have a designated office in your store or do you work at the cashwrap desk? If you don't have a clear and private area for paperwork, your concentration may often be disturbed. If it's impossible to create an office in your store, it might be possible to elongate your wrap desk. An extra 3 feet could be enough to put a laptop computer on a desk-like surface with two file cabinets underneath. The face of the "office desk" should match your cashwrap desk exactly. Of course, whenever a customer comes in the store your focus will be diverted, but that's the inherent situation of a small shop.

Clutter

If you don't know where to put something, does it end up in the office? Does everything end up there that doesn't have a home? Are you housing returns, holiday decorations, broken sign holders (that you plan to fix one day), outdated vendor catalogs and the like? There are few people so organized that their offices are clean and clear of clutter. To criticize a retailer's office clutter would be unfairly judgmental. While the topic of clutter is not "old school" Feng Shui, it certainly relates to modern retail issues.

Mental health care practitioners, when working with people who have big decisions to make or who are feeling overwhelmed in their lives, have been known to say, "Clean out a drawer!" You can try this at home. Clean out your sock or underwear drawer and see how you feel. It sounds basic and corny yet it's a simple, powerful, short-term transformational tool. A clear space allows room for new thoughts, new opportunities – new socks – to come into your life.

Now imagine a clean, clutter-free office. It may take a bit. First you might visualize all the things you need to clean up and throw out. Then you'll wonder when you'll ever have the time to do that. Next you'll think this whole concept is crazy or a waste of time and you'll hang some Chinese coins on a red thread over your computer and hope for the best.

Clearing the clutter from your office, stockroom, toilet and the entire store is a form of renovation. It reenergizes the entire space and makes room for new stock, new opportunities and new customers. When you clear clutter, you also clean house – always an important aspect to good sales.

Of course like anything good in retail, it takes time and effort. Putting in this effort is a form of positive thinking and manifesting better business. Try to think of clearing clutter as a form of display. You know that takes time and most often it pays off. So will clearing, cleaning and organizing.

Several years ago, a storeowner who was constantly miserable at work and wanted me to figure out why, called me. When I arrived, she took me on a tour of her lovely store. I couldn't see anything wrong with her visual merchandising, store flow, image or merchandise. Then I got lucky. She told me that the ceiling felt "heavy" to her.

I went to the attic of the building that was directly over her store and it was filled with furniture. I asked her where the furniture came from and she replied, "My first marriage – I'm just storing it here." I asked if the furniture held bad memories for her, and she said, "Yes, it was an awful marriage and a very angry divorce." When I asked why she was saving the furniture, she replied that she hoped to give it to her son for his first apartment when he graduated from college in two years.

Manmade things absorb and retain the energy that surrounds them. The furniture held old, sad, angry memories and energetically felt "heavy" overhead. As soon as she removed the furniture and placed it in storage outside the store, she felt happier and lighter at work.

Office Layout

A legend in the Wild West, James Butler "Wild Bill" Hickok was killed by Jack McCall in Deadwood, Dakota, on August 2, 1876. Hickok was shot in the back of the head the one (and reputed only) time he sat with his back to the door. No one feels comfortable with his or her back to the door. It's a vulnerable position that can make you feel uneasy. Have you ever been so focused at your desk that you've been startled by someone sneaking up behind you?

Most likely they weren't sneaking at all, but because you couldn't see them, you were unaware of their presence. If at all possible, position your desk so you can see out your door. If there's no door, make sure your back is not toward the entry into the room.

The bottom line is that you should be able to instantly see people coming into your workspace. If that's impossible, position a mirror so that it acts like the rear-view mirror in a car. Mount it on the wall so you can see movement behind you. Try to make sure that you don't see yourself in the mirror. We are often so self-critical that constantly seeing ourselves can be more annoying than we need on a moment-to-moment basis.

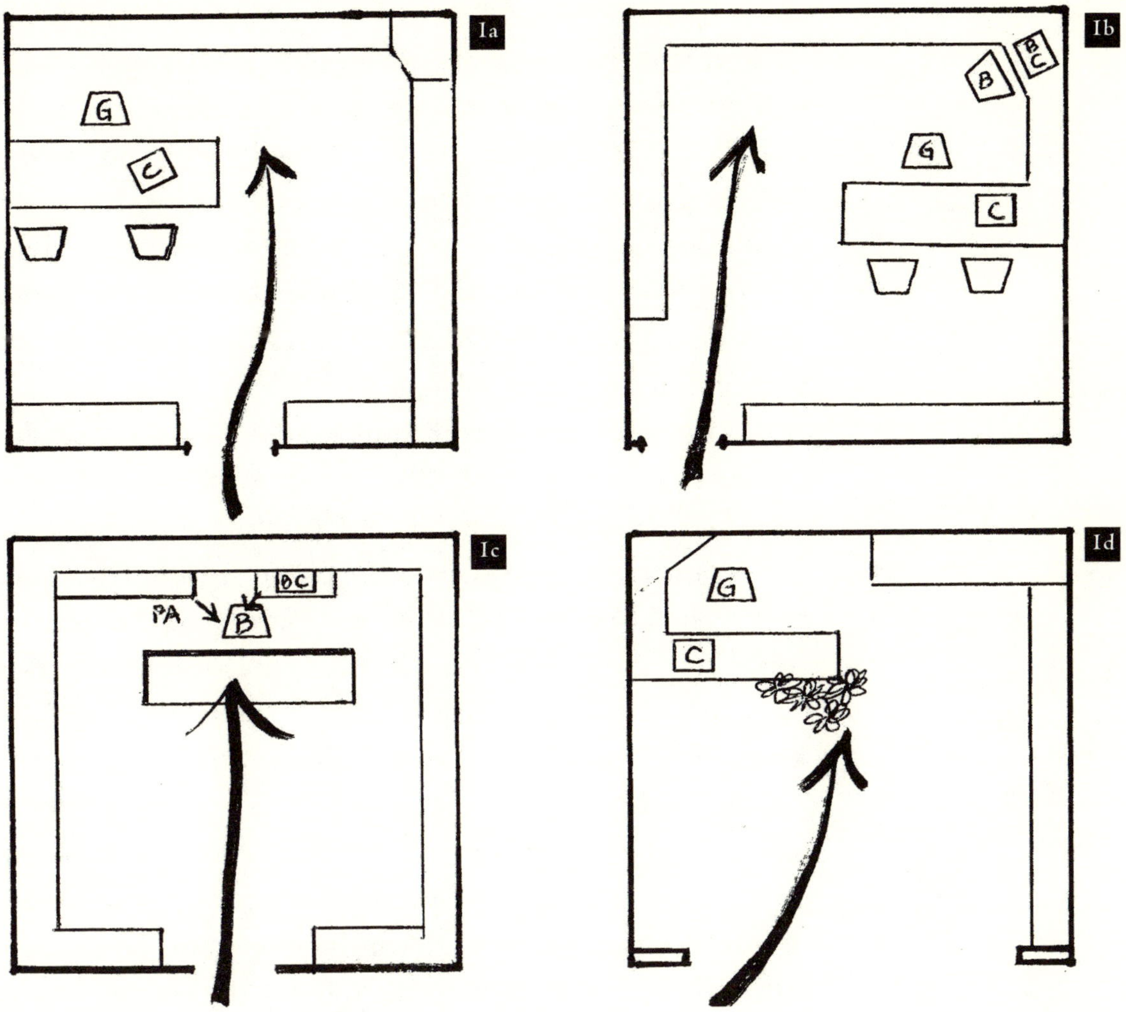

G = good chair location B = bad chair location PA = poison arrow created by corner
C = computer BC = bad computer placement

Ia - Good desk set-up, no poison arrows and the manager is always facing out without being in line with the door.
Ib - This shows two possible locations for the computer. If it goes in the corner, the person's back is to the door which will cut down on productivity over time.
Ic - Bad location for the desk. Energy rushes in and person always feels exposed. Poison arrows can "attack" from desk corners.
Id - This open door plan puts the desk in the corner while a plant blocks incoming potentially negative energy.

Behind you

Look at what is behind you as you sit at your desk. Whatever is behind you is what is energetically "backing you up." If you have neat files behind you, organization and vendors back you up. If behind you are open shelves filled with unsold or damaged stock, you are being backed up by disappointments and financial loss. Open shelves create poison arrows into your back. Hanging a curtain over open shelving is a solution to this problem.

What will work behind you? Vendor catalogs, new merchandise, any art or photos of positive forces in your life including your hobbies, family or friends. If you are angry or disappointed in any person in a photo, remove the photo from your workspace until the issue is resolved. Every time you glance at the photo or even in its direction, it will rekindle, albeit briefly, the negative emotion. You don't need that when you're trying to get work done.

Back yourself up with a picture of a mountain. Avoid pictures of water behind your chair.

Lillian Too suggests that you place a painting or photograph of a mountain behind your desk chair. Symbolically, a mountain protects and supports you. Don't hang any images of water or water flowing down the mountain. This kind of water imagery behind you (or your store) symbolizes lost opportunities.

Another great image to place behind you is a photograph of the façade of your bank's head office. It's always nice to be backed up by your bank!

In front of you

The images in front of you influence your present state of mind and represent your future. If you can get a screensaver on your computer that shows gold coins or positive money images, great! Any art or photographic image that symbolizes what you want your life to be like is perfect for the wall facing your desk.

Case study: There was a huge amount of stress and unease when I was corporate director of visual merchandising for a chain of Kohl's wannabes in the Northeast. I never felt a moment of peace or enjoyment in the position and I now realize that the huge screen-print of a ferocious, growling Bengal tiger facing me all day wasn't helping. It was free from a printing company and the colors and graphics were great. I should have known better. Now you do!

Below you

Soft surfaces are more comfortable for your feet. If you tend to kick off your shoes while at your desk, carpeting is preferable to cold cement, wood, vinyl or tile. You can find an attractive remnant or area rug that makes you feel good about your space. Just remember to vacuum it at least once a week.

Above you

Any type of ceiling is fine as long as it's consistent. If you have suspended ceiling tiles, they should be clean and unbroken. Open areas in a suspended ceiling above your seat are negative for your energy. There is always the sense of dust and debris falling onto your head.

Any beams over your head compress your energy and you will experience headaches and illness over time. Move the desk so you're not under the beam. If that's not possible, look for remedies to the problem in Chapter Nine.

Skylights, while fabulous on the selling floor, are considered to be negative when directly overhead. There is always the feeling of vulnerability. Again, move your desk. Having a recessed ceiling light shining directly onto your head is also negative. Not only will your head heat up, but the light will throw shadows on your workspace. You will always feel "in the way" in your own space.

Your desk

Don't "make do" for your desk. You don't want to feel mildly disappointed when you sit down to work. Your desk must be large enough for you to work on comfortably. There should be enough clear space underneath the desk so you can stretch your legs out easily. The height, depth and width should work for your needs. The desk doesn't have to be expensive or fancy but should be sturdy and comfortable. Customers will most likely never see the desk, so it doesn't make sense to invest a lot of money in a new desk unless you have the money and it would make you happy.

Keep it as clutter-free as possible. Clean areas on your desk allow for clear thoughts. Buying a used desk can cause problems. All things hold energy, and if an unsuccessful retailer previously owned the desk, the depressed energy it contains will still be in the desk. Buy a used desk only from a successful person. If you don't know the desk's history, clear its energy by "smoking it" with cedar and sage. Mix cedar shavings with sage from your spice cabinet in a small frying pan. Ignite the mix and then blow out the flame, allowing it to smolder. The smoke is cleansing.

Under you

Your ideal chair is sturdy, supportive and comfortable. It has a full back with armrests. The full back mimics the power and support of a symbolic mountain behind you – the ideal situation for any home or business.

Don't sit on a broken chair. It's bad luck and annoying – not a great combination. It's just like a broken drawer. Every time you open the drawer or even think of opening it, you feel a tinge of annoyance. "Why haven't I fixed this?" you wonder, and then start a mental list of why you haven't had the time, money, energy, skill or know-how to get the job done. Once you've finished your millisecond list of negatives, your mood has shifted slightly in a negative direction. Get it done as quickly as possible. It will pay off through improved moods and productivity.

Lighting

While overhead fluorescent lighting is the standard in most non-selling spaces, you can improve your office immeasurably by purchasing a table lamp for your desk. Don't work under fluorescent lights, which are cold and irritating and vibrate at a high rate of speed that is invisible to most people but can affect the nervous system in the long run. If you can, unscrew the fluorescent bulbs over your desk and instead, plug all incandescent lamps you need to read easily and feel comfortable. Use full-spectrum or "daylight" bulbs to make your desk area even more comfortable. If by some miracle you have a large office, it's still not desirable to have fluorescent lights anywhere near your desk.

Denise Linn originated the Feng Shui system called "interior alignment." She has authored nine books and lectures extensively around the world. The following is excerpted from her book, *Sacred Space*, Ballantine Books, 1995.

Tips for Creating Good Fortune in Your Office

For insight, place books in your office so they are visible when you first enter the room.
For clarity, place wind chimes inside the door.
For peace of mind, place the desk so you can see the door. Traditional Feng Shui advocates avoiding being in a direct line with the door, but your own intuition is best.

To increase prosperity, pay attention to the wealth corner of your desk and office.
To bring more love into your office, place a round mirror on the wall.
To increase good luck, place a bowl of flowers on your desk.
To clear work blockages, unblock the doorway and move objects stored behind doors.
To invite opportunity in, oil squeaky or sticky doors and doorknobs. Clean your entrance door until it sparkles.
To expand your vistas and open your creativity, clear your desk.

The Stockroom

To make this short and sweet – keep it clean and neat. Start by adding shelves all the way up to the ceiling. Store your rarely used items on the highest shelves. This includes seasonal display trim and signage, rarely used odd-sized boxes and other items you don't mind climbing a ladder to retrieve. In the middle area are all the everyday or frequently used items, with the heavy, large items stocked below.

Put on clearance or donate old stock that hasn't sold in more than a year. Be merciless! You bought it, it didn't sell, get over it and get rid of it. Having merchandising failures taking up valuable stock space is a drain on your emotional energy. Fluorescent lights are fine for this area, but make sure they emit adequate light.

Energy stagnates in poorly lit or dark areas. As your stockroom is probably in the money, fame or relationships area of your store, stagnant energy is the last thing you need. Energize these areas by cleaning out, straightening up and making sure the lighting is bright for visual clarity.

If your lease includes an overhead or basement stockroom, make it as clean, organized and well lit as those on the main floor. The floor above your selling floor can feel oppressive when it's dark, dirty and disorganized with old stock. A similar situation in the basement stockroom gives no energetic support to the selling floor. It can drain the life from the store.

Restrooms

There is no good area for a toilet in a store according to the principals of Feng Shui. If you have a choice in placement when building out a store, the best solution is to position one between two sections of the Bagua. Never have a toilet in the center of the store or near the front door. The center of your store represents balance and health – too important to go down the drain. Unconscious fear results from a toilet by the front door. As toilets are an essential part of life, there are many remedies to make them less unlucky. Please note they cannot become lucky in any way – just less inauspicious.

No matter where your restroom is located, take the following steps to ensure that it doesn't drain energy from your store:

1. Keep the door closed at all times.

2. If you have a toilet seat, keep it down.

3. Install a mirror on the inside of the bathroom door facing into the restroom.

4. If the toilet seat is facing your desk or the wrap desk, install a mirror the height and width of the toilet on the wall directly across from the toilet. It should reflect the toilet completely so it will be at floor level rising to the height of the toilet.

5. Do not decorate the restroom. It increases the bad luck. Keep it clean, uncluttered, simple and well lit. If you (kindly)

allow customers to use it, add a chair or bench for their handbags or parcels.

6. Keep the room as small as possible as long as it complies with ADA regulations.

7. If the restroom is large and it shares a wall with your office or with the main selling floor, add floor-to-ceiling shelves along that wall to act as an energetic buffer between the toilet and a work area. Stock spare fixture hardware, extra bags, etc., on the shelves and cover it with an attractive curtain or with mirrored sliding doors.

Hallways

Hallways connect essential back areas of your store. They become temporary stockrooms when something either doesn't have a home or is too large to fit on a shelf. Cluttered hallways create poison arrows, which make walking through them uncomfortable. Remember: Your goal is to reduce the discomfort level in your store. Having you and your staff "dodge" sliding signs, sharp fixture edges or other miscellaneous debris while you try to get to the back door or office lowers the positive energy in the store. It also creates irritability, which is never good for customer interactions.

Lighting in your halls is as vital as on the selling floor, so light them up! Fluorescents are fine. But dark hallways depress the overall energy of the store. It doesn't matter that "no one can see them." They exist in your space and affect your store equally with the "seen" spaces.

Feng Shui Magic by Lillian Too

Lillian Too is the internationally renowned author of numerous books on Feng Shui. She is an expert in The Compass

School, which works with direction rather than the placement of the front door. In *Lillian Too's Irresistible Book of Feng Shui Magic* (Element Books, 2001), she offers insights into some ways to make your office and back spaces more profitable.

The Money Tree: Money trees are available online or at many stores carrying Chinese merchandise. They are small trees with gold trunks and limbs. The more expensive trees are made with real gold wire with semiprecious stones hanging as leaves. You can make your own lucky money tree. Your intention is what counts. Be creative and create a tree of your own with coins and semiprecious stones attached with red thread or ribbons. The tree belongs in the wealth section of your office.

The Laughing Buddha: The fat, happy Buddha is also known as the Buddha of Wealth. He symbolically absorbs problems and stress, allowing your day to run more smoothly and with more joy. Find a statue of this Buddha that makes you smile and place it so it faces the doorway of your office.

Coins: Feng Shui practitioners often use ancient Chinese coins (or reproductions) to symbolize prosperity, success and luck. Chinese coins are round with square holes in their centers. These coins represent the balance of heaven and earth. Tied together with red and gold thread or ribbons, they can be placed on your cash register, computer or phone, or in your invoice books or checkbooks. You can also use silver dollars for a more American flair, but the Chinese coins hold more symbolic value.

REVIEW

Chapter Eight: Non-Selling Spaces and Feng Shui

1. In Feng Shui, your **non-selling spaces** are as important as the selling floor. The energy generated by unseen areas influences all aspects of your store's success.

2. Your **office** is the heart of your store. You should feel refreshed, reenergized, alert and calm. If you don't feel any of these things, it's time to rethink the space.

3. Clearing the **clutter** from your office, stockroom, toilet and the entire store is a form of renovation.

4. **Manmade things** absorb and retain the energy that surrounds them. Remove objects and fixtures that hold negative energy. Your attic, basement and unseen areas should not store any fixtures from failed businesses.

5. Don't work with your **back to the door**. Add an incandescent light to your desk.

6. Energy stagnates in **poorly lit or dark areas**. As your stockroom, office or bathroom are probably in the money, fame or relationships area of your store, energize these areas by cleaning out, straightening up and making sure the lighting is bright for visual clarity.

7. If you have a choice in the placement of a bathroom when building out a store, the best solution is to position one between two sections of the Bagua. Never have a **toilet** in the center of the store or near the front door.

8. **Lighting** in your halls is as vital as on the selling floor. Light them up! Fluorescents are fine. Dark hallways depress the overall energy of the store. It doesn't matter that "no one can see them!" They exist in your space and affect your store equally with the "seen" spaces.

9. Use a **money tree** in the wealth sector of your office or store. If you purchase one, make sure the "leaves" of the tree are made of jade, rose quartz, semi-precious stones or real coins. Don't skimp. Buy a money tree that represents what you want for the future - not what you're making in the present.

10. Place a **laughing Buddha** so it is facing the doorway of your office. If you choose to have more than one, put one facing you as you sit at your desk. For absorbing extra problems, place a laughing Buddha behind your seat as well.

11. Tie together **nine Chinese coins** with a narrow red ribbon or thick red thread. Keep these coins on or in your account book or in your stores' check book. Any multiple of nine is good luck. If you want to do a chain of 18 or 27 coins you will add to the power of the concept.

12. J. Jill uses built-in painted wood bins to house all their extra small fixture parts. They are well-labeled and organized. The bins are built into the stockroom or bathroom on a wall and allow fixture changes to be simple and quick. This is an excellent use of stockroom or bathroom space.

9

Clearings, Cures and Remedies with Intention

For realtors, it's all about location, location, location. For retailers, it's all about intention, intention, intention. When working with Black Sect Feng Shui, it's important to start with what you want to achieve, your intention for your life and your store. Once that's clear, you can focus on making it a reality.

For every problem there is a cure or remedy. This chapter lists some basic cures, problems and their solutions.

Getting Started

- Before you implement a cure or remedy, you need to focus on three things:
  1. Be very clear about what you want to happen. Clarity counts.
  2. Have a strong wish for it to work.
  3. Feel it happen in the present and believe in your power to create positive change.

- Take action. Cures and remedies succeed once you do the work to make things happen. It is necessary that your intention always be visualized using positive images and words. Attach no negative thoughts or expressions to your visualization. See your desire for your store manifest in complete detail. Be specific and imagine it happening in the moment.

A powerful affirmation is: "Customers are in my store and each person is purchasing $1,000 (or whatever amount works best for you – don't skimp) worth of merchandise, which they will keep and enjoy." The negative version is: "I need more customers to come into my store, buy a lot and not make any returns."

According to Professor Lin Yun, the founder of Black Sect Feng Shui, there are two very important tips for visualization:

1. Visualize in detail. See your desire occurring in as much detail as possible.
2. Visualize in three stages.
   a. See the beginning – the start of what you want.

b. See the middle – the continuation and improvement of your desire.
c. See the culmination – the positive achievement of your desire.

Moving into a New Store

There is nothing like the rush of energy you feel when moving into a new store. It excites, energizes, stresses and exhausts you. A fresh, clean, just-built store is open to all possibilities. No matter how crazed and busy you are, know your intention for the new store.

Intention = your goal, objective, plan, aim, purpose or target.

Before you move into your new store, plan some time to take the following steps.

1. *Define the purpose of your job.* Understanding your purpose at work will give your higher self a blueprint to work with. Your intention of your purpose at work will help you achieve your desires.

2. *Define your store's image and intent.* What do you want your store to communicate to others – and to you?

3. *Clean absolutely everything.* Clean the inside and outside of your store, the walls, the fixtures (if they are used either by you or some other store), the stock areas, basement and attic, restrooms, windows, floors and ceilings. Ceilings and walls need not be cleaned in a brand-new store unless fine dust has settled throughout the store. Use lemon water for your cleansing. Squeeze a lemon into a gallon of water or add rinds from

three lemons. As you are cleaning, repeat either silently or out loud: This is my store. Its energy is clean and clear.

4. *Make sure everything works.* Fix anything that is broken or working poorly. If something serves no function, get rid of it. Even a phone machine that has poor voice quality will be energetically perceived as you and your store being unclear and unprofessional.

5. *Perform a store blessing.* You can smoke the store using cedar and sage or sprinkle salt into the four corners of the store – and in the corners throughout the store. Say a prayer of your choice. A simple prayer would be: Please bless this store and all who work and shop here. Make it a happy, healthy and prosperous place to work and make each and every transaction a positive blessing for our customers and us.

Moving into a Previously Owned or Leased Store

Space clearing becomes even more important when you move into a store that was previously occupied. Energy – both good and bad – gets left behind when tenants move out. It makes sense to dedicate a period of time to clearing the new space energetically. Again, with thanks to Denise Linn:

1. *Do a complete cleaning.* (See #3 above.)

2. *Name your store.* The store has its formal, public name that is a vital part of the naming ceremony. You might hold another, private naming ritual to add your own name onto the formal name. The format of this ceremony is personal and up to you.

3. *Moving-in Ceremony.* This ceremony is designed to formally announce to the spirit of the store – and to the higher selves

of you and your staff – that you are moving into this space for the success and well-being of all involved.

You might run into skeptics among your staff. That's very understandable. These ceremonies might sound odd to people who haven't been exposed to the concepts. Don't insist that everyone attend a ritual or ceremony. It's preferable to have people there who appreciate the moment rather than those who feel resentment, consternation or anger.

Entrance Energy Cures

David Daniel Kennedy's book, *Feng Shui Tips for a Better Life* (Storey Publishing, 1998), delves deeply into cures and remedies based on Lin Yun's teachings. Below are some concepts from his book that I've modified for retailers.

1. *Remove the blocks to your entrance.* One of the first things to do when moving into a store – or in your existing space – is to expand and clear the pathways that lead into your store. That means removing anything that blocks your entrance. For example, before you lease a space in a mall, find out if the space immediately in front of your entryway is up for lease as well. The last thing you need when moving into a space is to find a model car parked in front of your store blocking the energy from entering.

2. *Make sure your front door is in great condition and is easy to open and close.* You don't want "stuck energy" as the introduction to your store.

3. *Make sure your name, street number, phone number and hours are easy to find and read.* Too often, retailers rely on their overhead signs to tell customers who they are. When people walk down a street, they rarely look up at the overhead signs. They are looking at the store at eye level. It's vital that your store name

be repeated at eye level somewhere on the face of your store. Your hours and phone number can go on your door in vinyl letters. They can be small as long as they're legible. The street number is usually found over the front door.

4. *Make sure your front door opens completely.* Doors that open less than 90 degrees symbolize being less open to wealth and opportunities.

5. *Clear all the space around your front door area.*

6. *Hang metal wind chimes on or near the front door to welcome in customers.* Do not hang the chimes so the customers have to duck to avoid being hit in the head. While this might seem obvious, it's easy to become overzealous with remedies. The wind chimes should be clean, sound harmonious and hang from a red ribbon or cord that is 9 inches (or a multiple of 9 inches) long.

7. *Symbolically "seed" the path to your front door.* You can use birdseed or money buried in the dirt on the way into your store. If you are in a mall, this will obviously not work. You might be able to hide pennies in the small spaces on the façades of neighboring stores or in the planters in the middle of the mall. To avoid being seen, you might want to do this very early in the morning!

8. *Banners waving in the wind attract positive attention to your store and front door.* OMO, Norma Kamali on West 56th Street in New York City has three metallic gold fabric banners fluttering in front of her store. They attract very positive attention and are a landmark on the street. Without much advertising or publicity, she has successfully been in business for many years.

Feng Shui Tools and Cures

It's important that you give a lot of thought to what is working in your store and what needs to be "cured." Don't just slap a mirror onto a wall and hope for the best. Remember to pay attention to what you're doing. Your intention and attention are a vital part of the process and its success. Believing in the cure aids in its power as does visualizing the desired results. Bottom line – keep a good, conscious attitude. Some successful cures include:

Aquariums: You should put an aquarium either in the wealth, entrance or career section of your store. The ideal number of fish is nine or a multiple of nine. While any colors of fish are fine, orange is less lucky while red and black are considered to be more auspicious. David Kennedy suggests eight red and one black fish. If a fish dies, replace it immediately. It is believed that the dead fish soaked up the bad luck meant for the owner of the store.

Aquarium with gold coins on the bottom of the tank with live gold fish.

Add nine, 18 or – better yet – 27 gold coins to the bottom of your fish tank. They can be real or fake as long as they will remain gold under water. This will energize your aquarium for even more prosperity. Visualize the fish, water and tank bringing you the prosperity you desire.

Fountains: The best place for a fountain in the wealth area of your store (the far left ninth) or in the front, career area of the store. The water should flow into the store toward the cash register. Don't create an outdoor fountain with water flowing away from your store – and sending blessings and prosperity across the street. The fountain can be any size, shape or material but a natural material is best. You don't

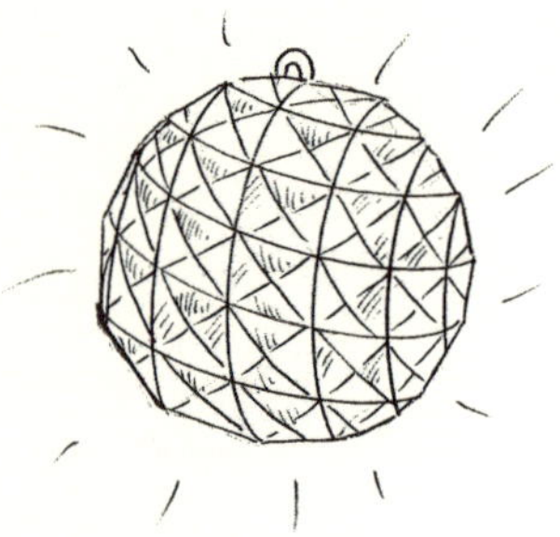

Cut crystal ball.

have to keep the fountain on after store hours. Fix or replace a broken fountain to maintain the good luck. When you install the fountain, visualize that money is flowing into your cash register and checking account.

Crystals: Use crystals as a Feng Shui remedy. The ideal crystals for remedies are round, at least 1½ inches in diameter and multifaceted. If they work with your décor, hang the crystals on red thread, cord or ribbon in 9-inch lengths; 27 inches is considered to be very powerful as it's nine energized three times.

The front door aligned with the back door is a classic negative position. From the ceiling near the front door, hang a crystal above the front door and well above your customers' heads. (You don't want your customers to have to dodge hanging crystals.) The crystal will softly diffuse the flow of positive energy in the store before it flows out the back door.

Front windows aligned with back windows require the same remedy as above. Hang a crystal in either the front or back window. If a crystal in your front window doesn't work for your window display theme, the back window will work equally well.

Exposed overhead beams that are positioned over your desk or where salespeople stand at the checkout area will compress energy over time, causing illness and headaches. An exposed beam might also feel dangerous in an area prone to earthquakes. If you hang a crystal ball from a 9-inch red cord at each end of the beam, it will energetically disperse the negative energy.

Poison arrows created by sharp corners of walls, fixtures or doors can be softened by hanging a crystal from the top of the wall, fixture or door. Of course, the crystal might bounce around as people walk past, so it's not the ideal solution for a busy area. A round-leafed plant will soften a poison arrow corner just as well and might work better with your décor.

Light: One of the most valuable tools for curing problems in your store is lighting. Dark areas create stagnant energy that eventually kills sales over time. Bright lights are often used to redirect attention from a negative to a positive. For example, an exposed overhead beam hanging over the checkout area unconsciously creates a sense of unease.

Directing a spotlight on a great display next to where your customers are standing will redirect the negative thoughts of being trapped under a wood beam to "that's kind of great, I think I'll buy it."

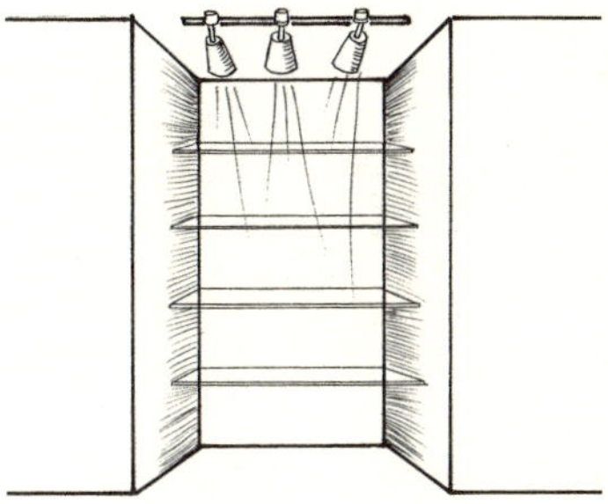

Light up nooks and crannies.

Cramped areas feel more spacious and take on new life when illuminated from above. **Nooks and crannies,** when lit up, become ideal areas for special classifications. A double-headed ceiling-mounted spotlight is affordable and will pay off quickly with increased sales.

Low overhead beams, valances or very low ceilings lose their oppressive energy when lighted from below. Low-wattage floodlights trained on the low ceiling will reduce the negative impact. Low-wattage wall-mounted spotlights trained on the bottom of the beam or valance will do the same. **Low ceilings** feel higher when light bounces back from inset fluorescent fixtures. **Columns** lit from above, below or within glow rather than feel like obstacles.

Crossed bamboo flutes: This is a traditional cure for slowing down rushing energy or alleviating negative energy from overhead beams. Two flutes, tied together with red ribbon or cord so that they are slanted toward each other at the top, will lift bad chi energy from an overhead beam or slow down rushing hallway energy. If you don't feel that these flutes have the right "look" for your store, other remedies are listed to cure the same problems using light, crystals, plants and wind chimes.

Wind chimes: These are sometimes called "dispersing cures" because they stop energy from moving too quickly down an aisle, hall or pathway. Good quality wind chimes give out a lovely sound. According to Lillian Too, "Do not hang metal wind chimes in east or southeast as these are wood corners. Instead, hang bamboo wind chimes in these corners." Although this book is based on Black Hat Feng Shui, and bringing in different schools and systems might confuse you, it is easy to buy the wind chimes in the correct material for the specific area that needs a cure. "Metal wind chimes should be hung in the west and northwest, while ceramic wind chimes can be hung in the southwest and northeast." Lillian Too also recommends that if you use a wind chime to deflect negative energy created by poison arrows, hang a hollow five-rod metallic wind chime, and it's even better if it has the design of a pagoda on top.

Wind dancers or banners: Often used to fill large, open spaces created by high ceilings, banners are the most common form of wind dancers found in retail environments. In East and West Asian countries, wind dancers, sometimes known as "danglers," are used extensively to create more exciting energy or chi in the store. They take the form of masses of hanging signs and can seem overwhelming to a person used to clear, uncluttered ceilings.

Banners don't have to be printed. You can use the colors that work with the section or direction of the department to create fresh energy in that area or to enhance a cure. For example, Terah Kathryn Collins writes: "A rich royal purple banner hung from a high ceiling in the Wealth area adds a three-dimensional point of interest, as well as a constant reminder of prosperity and abundance."

Of course, banners are also great for introducing new products or promotions. When you use banners outside your store, you attract attention and create positive energy. It pays to have banners created specifically for your store and its image. Hanging premade pastel banners of flowers or kittens might seem sweet but unless they represent your store's image, they can harm your sales rather than help them. If you are selling more upscale, sophisticated items, consider three, six or nine solid-colored banners – perhaps in an interesting metallic or textured material. They need not say anything. Just the movement and color are enough to attract positive chi into your store.

Wind dancers can be whirligigs or mobiles hung throughout your store. They are a symbolic cure rather than a traditional Feng Shui remedy. For example, a mobile of flying angels in the Helpful People area symbolizes our being looked after by those on the other side and the helpfulness of those in our lives on Earth.

Anything hanging from the ceiling should not energetically block access to merchandise. Unless the banners are hung over fixtures, their bottom should be a minimum of 7 feet from the floor. You don't want your customers to have to bob and weave to avoid getting hit in the head by your lucky mobile!

Plants and flowers: Connecting us to the outdoors and to the earth, plants and flowers bring positive energy into any store. They can be silk or real as long as they are lush, healthy and clean. Nurturing dying plants back to life in your store deadens the energy wherever they are located. Conversely, a dying plant will bring negative luck to the section of the Bagua where it's located.

Dried flowers have a dead energy. They might be used in combination with silks but on their own, their energy is dim at best. Also, they cannot be cleaned and often become faded dust collectors long before they are thrown out. Look for plants with rounded, non-pointy leaves. Pointed leaves create poison arrows and are considered unlucky. That goes double for most cacti.

Some good plants for your store include Scheffleara, philodendron, pothos, jade, croton, Chinese evergreen, peace lily (spathiphyllum), ficus, ivy, and most dracaenas, ferns and palms. Also on the "yes" list are blooming plants, which are excellent alternatives to fresh flowers. These include begonia, chrysanthemum, gloxinia, African violets, kalanchoe, Gerbera daisy and cyclamen." (Thank you to Terah Kathryn Collins, author of *Home Design With Feng Shui A-Z*, Hay House, Inc., 1999.)

Great photo or painting for the marriage area.

Paintings, prints, photographs and sculptures: These are all symbolic cures and enhancements for different areas of your store. Artwork in your store should always have positive themes and ideally relate on a symbolic level to the section in which it's hung:

Marriage and Relationships: Art that represents two of anything – two ducks, two jars, two people, two trees and so on – are ideal for this area. Peonies are also considered to be fortunate for the romance area. This section relates to business partnerships as well.

Wealth: A painting of a sailing ship with its sails filled with wind (wealth energy) represents opportunity and unforeseen riches. It's even better if the ship is loaded with gold coins. Of course, you can imagine it is filled with coins even if you can't see them.

Any piece of art that represents a dragon is extremely powerful. In The Compass School, dragons belong in the east area of your store. You might want to use them in both sections if they are in different areas. Each type of dragon represents something different in the ancient Chinese tradition. Dragons can bring excitement, change and growth. In this wealth area, any positive images that represent wealth to you will symbolically enhance the space.

Fame: This is a great area to repeat your store's name. It is also perfect for images of recognition that appeal to you personally. If an image of the sun means fame to you, use that image in your store. A bouquet of flowers is thrown onto the stage in thanks for a great performance. A photo or painting of this image will remind you every time you look in that direction of your desire for recognition – and the achievement of this desire.

Children and Creativity: Any image that represents creativity or actual children is perfect for this section.

Friends and Family: Images that represent humans and/or animals relating to each other in loving, positive ways are appropriate in this area. This is also a great area to honor your customers with some images that relate to them or, if appropriate, post a customer bulletin board.

Stew Leonard's in Norwalk, Connecticut, has a huge bulletin board filled with photographs of its customers in exotic locations holding Stew Leonard's shopping bags. People are always stopping at the board to see if they know anyone on display. It adds to the community flavor of the local, highly successful store.

Helpful People, Travel and Networking: Images of horses represent power, good fortune in opportunities, strength and speed. They are considered to be very lucky and would be great in the area where friends bring opportunities into your life.

Career: This area might be where your front door lies, so artwork might not be appropriate here. If there is space for art, a crane or horse image could be perfect. According to Sharon Stasney, author of the excellent book *Feng Shui Your Work Spaces* (Sterling Publishing, 2004), "The crane is a symbol for success with longevity. Although many business ventures can bring short-term profits, the crane represents the ability to realize long-lasting returns on an investment. Like cranes, pine trees are also a symbol of longevity and are known for being tenacious and enduring where other trees fail to grow."

Knowledge: This area represents your expertise as well as new knowledge flowing into your life and store. Appropriate images include a phoenix, elephants or an old, wise man.

Auspicious Patterns and Symbols*

Pattern	**Meaning**
Elephants	Wisdom
Pine trees	Longevity and endurance
Vase	Peace
Phoenix	Grace and wisdom
Fish	Success
Lotus	Endurance and uprightness
Water ripples	Wealth and heavenly blessings
Clouds	Heavenly blessings and wisdom
Gold pieces	Wealth
Yin-Yang	Unions and balance
Flowers	Prosperity and love
Tortoise	Longevity
Old coins	Wealth
Bats	Good luck
Cranes	Fidelity, honesty and longevity
Deer	Wealth and luck
Fu dogs	Protection and loyalty

* Evelyn Lip, Feng Shui for the Home, Heian International, 1990
* Nancy SantoPietro, Feng Shui: Harmony by Design, Berkley Publishing Group, 1996

Dragon	Power, authority and strength
Fruit	Good luck and health
Old man	Wisdom and longevity

Mirrors: Mirrors are an effective remedy for many different situations. The most important thing to remember about mirrors is that whatever they reflect will be doubled. For example, if your mirror reflects the bathroom, the negative energy from that area will double in strength. Reflecting traffic on the street magnifies the rushing energy passing your store. If you're doubling the jewelry in a case with a back mirror, you are, at the same time, also reflecting the customers walking by or standing in front of the counter. Mirrors can enhance or distract, so their correct use is vital to a store's success. Some points to keep in mind when placing mirrors in your store:

Mirrors should reflect the whole person to make people feel welcome and comfortable in your store. Don't symbolically cut off their heads or feet.

Clarity and reflection: It is important that a mirror reflects clear, solid images. Mirror squares, tiles, lots of beveled edges, broken shards (artsy but disturbing) or spotted surfaces distort and fracture the reflection. This distortion scatters the energy and produces the opposite of the desired cure or remedy. Instead of creating and reflecting good energy, these mirrors are splintering and scattering it, creating confusion and stress.

Mirrors and height: Mirrors should be hung so that people of almost every height can see their heads and feet at the same time. In a dressing room, make sure they start at the floor and go to at least 6½ feet high. The goal height for the mirrors should be as tall as your tallest customer. If your customers are taller than 6½ feet, go floor to ceiling. When you "cut off" people's heads, they don't feel welcome in your store. If you symbolically cut off your own head, there's no room (energetically) to grow.

Columns: Round columns are less of a problem than those that are square or rectangular. However, a wide, round column can block chi if it's located in an area that blocks your customers' view of the store. As a remedy, consider a round mirror mounted on the face of the column to symbolically create an opening in the support. To make the mirror work with your décor, one idea is to mount a small shelf underneath with any current promotional literature or product.

Square or rectangular columns have four sharp corners that create poison arrows. The most popular Feng Shui cure for columns is to mirror them on all four sides. Nancy SantoPietro suggests adding draped fabric or small, rounded, floor-to-ceiling Mylar columns on all four corners to further alleviate the negative corners.

Another option is to install standards on all four sides of the columns and then have rounded shelves cut to create circles of shelves resting on the brackets. Your merchandise will further dull the poison arrows.

If a wall blocks the entrance to your store or to a department, add a mirror to this wall to help the wall disappear. If the mirror reflects the front door, stairway or elevators, use art, photographs or attractive or informational graphics to divert attention from the wall.

Staircases: Staircases are hallways that go up and down. Energy can rush up or down without rest. People may feel slightly anxious going down stairs. Unfortunately, staircases in stores have the exact opposite effect of those in our homes. A staircase in a home offers relaxation potential, as the bedrooms are usually upstairs. In a store, the departments upstairs are often considered to be the less exciting areas. People dislike level changes and especially hate to climb stairs. Reward your customers for their efforts by adding artwork or great displays on the stairwell walls. The lighting in your stairwell should be bright and clear.

Stairs directly opposite your front door: Energy flows through your front door and down the stairs. In order to keep the energy on the first floor, place fixtures in the path of the energy flow. If you want people to go downstairs as well, create a clear aisle leading down but make it a secondary aisle. Give people a reason to go downstairs. Inform them with a clear sign what they will find down there. If they have to guess, they won't bother. And don't forget to light up the stairwell!

Add live or good silk plants underneath open stairways. Light up the plants with incandescent flood lights.

Stairs with open risers: These stairs make people unconsciously nervous. They are not welcoming and can be dangerous. If you have a choice, install full-backed stairs. If you are stuck with open-backed stairs and you want to retain a modern feel, you might want to screw frosted Lucite to the back of the stairwell. The light will shimmer through and the stairs will feel more solid and safe. A less sleek option is filling the open areas in with hanging plants.

Too many windows: You have too many windows when you start running out of wall space and begin complaining about the wasted space in your windows. Large windows require displays as well as great visuals within the store. Your entire store becomes a display with too many windows. Some remedies for this problem are:

Mirrored armoires: A mirrored armoire sitting in the window but facing into the store will reflect the energy of your store back into the space. Cover the back of the armoire with fabric or artwork so people walking by can't see its unfinished back from the street. Try hanging a piece of fabric from the ceiling, behind the armoire, to the floor. The fabric becomes a temporary wall for a window display.

Use overhead grids with hanging fabric to create fake walls in windows.

Sheer fabric walls: Hanging semi-sheer fabric from the ceiling to the floor in sections of your windows will allow natural light in, while creating a backdrop for interesting displays. Use dowels for the top and bottom of each swath of fabric to keep it taut. Of course, iron or steam out any wrinkles. When customers notice wrinkles, they cease noticing your products on display.

Crystals: Hanging 1-inch-diameter crystals in the windows will capture energy flowing out and keep it in the store. They will also set up rainbows in your store. On the downside, make sure they don't blind pedestrians and drivers. Also, check to make sure they don't reflect onto anything flammable. Set them up but plan to move them if the sun's reflection makes them more of a danger than a remedy!

REVIEW

Chapter Nine: Clearings, Cures and Remedies with Intention

1. Before you **implement** a cure or remedy, you need to focus on three things:

4. Be very clear about what you want to happen. Clarity counts.

5. Have a strong wish for it to work.

6. Feel it happen in the present and believe in your power to create positive change.

Take action. Cures and remedies succeed once you do the work to make things happen.

2. It is necessary that your **intention** always be visualized using positive images and words. Attach no negative thoughts or expressions to your visualization.

3. See your desire for your store manifest in complete detail. Be *specific* and imagine it happening *in the moment.*

4. Know your intention for your store before you move in. Do a **space clearing** before you start fixturing the space.

5. **Clean** the inside and outside of your store, the walls, fixtures (if they are used either by you or some other store), stock areas, basement, attic, restrooms, windows, floors and ceilings where possible.

6. **Make sure everything works.** Fix anything that is broken or working poorly. If something serves no function, get rid of it.

7. **Perform a store blessing.** Bring your spiritual beliefs and faith into the blessing of your new store – or revitalize the energy of your existing store.

8. **Your front door:** Remove the **blocks** to your entrance.
- Make sure your front door is in great condition and is easy to open and close. You don't want "stuck energy" as the introduction to your store.
- Make sure your name, street number, phone number and hours are easy to find and read.
- Make sure your front door opens completely.
- Clear all the space around your front door area.
- Hang metal wind chimes on or near the front door to welcome in customers.

9. **Banners** waving in the wind attract positive attention to your store and front door.

10. **Paintings, prints, photographs and sculptures** are symbolic cures and enhancements for different areas of your store. Artwork in your store should always have positive themes and ideally relate on a symbolic level to the section in which it is hung.

10

Answers to Commonly Asked Questions

What about mirrors?

- Test a mirror before hanging it to make sure it reflects positive images.
- Don't hang mirrors directly across from each other – it creates confusion.
- Hang only solid mirrors. Mirror tiles or any type of broken image reflects negatively, and disturbs and distracts customers.
- Make sure mirrors are tall enough to leave room over a tall person's head and long enough to show his feet. Don't symbolically cut off any body parts!
- Don't hang mirrors so they reflect the front door – it sends the energy back out of the store.
- When you mirror cases, you double your product. Make sure you're not doubling street traffic rushing by your store as well.

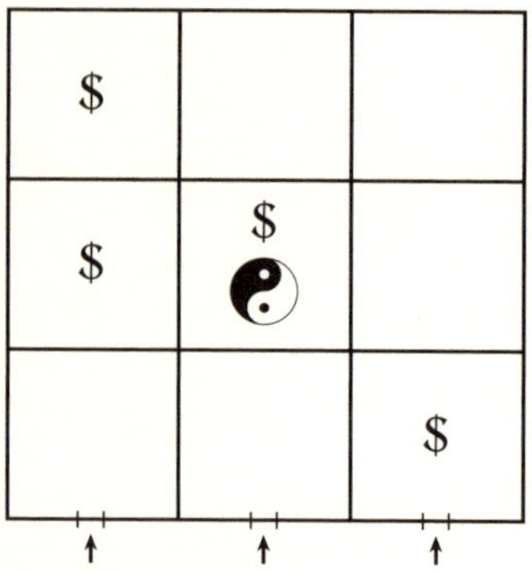

Best places for register.

Where is the best place for the register or registers?

The money section of your store is in the far left ninth of your total floor plan. If that ninth is located in a stockroom or toilet, the next best area is in the far left ninth of your selling floor. The left middle section of your store – Friends and Family – is a good choice as well. If you are able to keep the register area very clean and organized, the center of the store, the center of balance and health is also positive.

Another good area is in the front far right ninth of your store – the helpful people, travel and networking section. This only works if your front door is not in that area. You don't want customers to walk directly into the cashwrap area.

Your salespeople need to be able to work and have full visibility of the store at the same time. They should not have to work with their backs to the selling floor or front door.

How about dressing rooms?

Dressing rooms must be lit adequately with incandescent, not fluorescent light. It is far more flattering and will aid in sales. If you have overhead fluorescent lights, remove the bulbs and replace them with incandescent lights. Lights mounted 5½ feet from the floor will throw soft light around most people's faces and less around their bodies, making the shopping experience more pleasurable.

Dressing rooms ought to have a bench or chair to welcome customers and help them to feel comfortable. Avoid poison arrows by building a bench in the corner or between two walls. There should also be a full door or full curtain that closes easily and completely to give customers a sense of privacy and safety. Dressing rooms work best when they don't face the front door of your store.

Provide enough sturdy hooks or bars to hold all the merchandise to be tried on, as well as the customers' clothing and

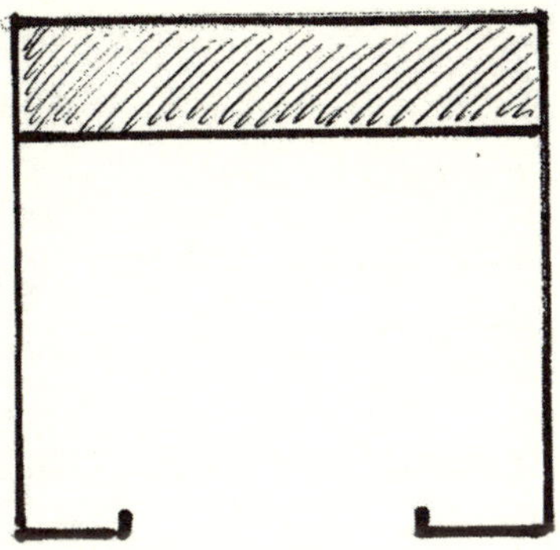

1. Good Bench.

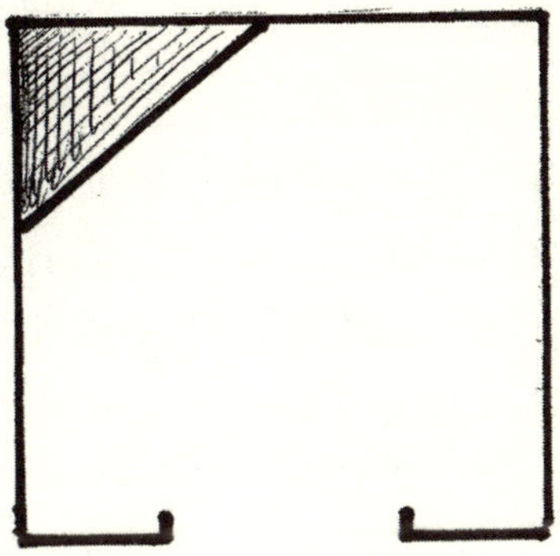

2. Angled bench doesn't create poison arrows.

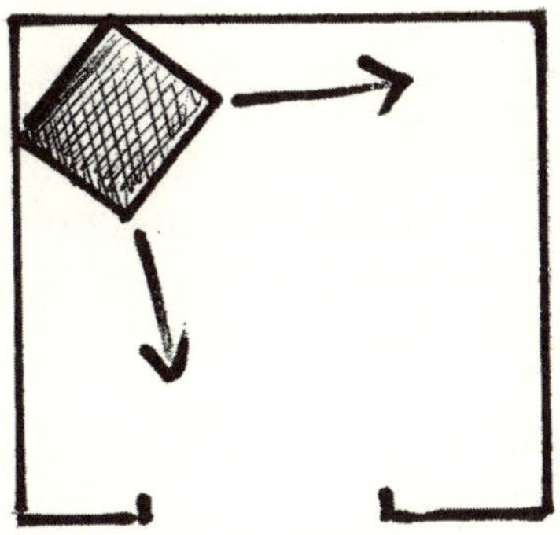

3. Cube or square chains create poison arrows

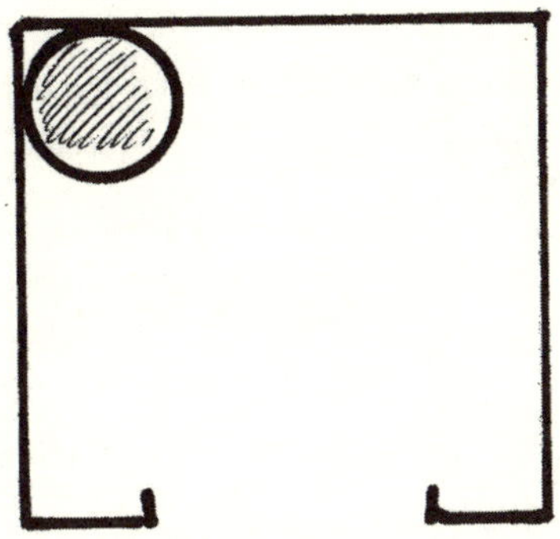

4. Round chairs soften the energy.

bags. Soft shades of off white with a warm base such as vanilla, baby pink, cream or peach are all perfect for dressing rooms. Aim to flatter all skin tones.

Mirrors ideally are sized from the floor to at least 61/2 feet high to accommodate all heights. Have the largest dressing rooms possible for your store. Space equals quality to the customer and that quality will be reflected onto the merchandise. The floors in the dressing rooms must be spotless!

The bathroom is in the money section. What do I do?

- Keep the door closed and the toilet seat down at all times. If the toilet doesn't have a seat, buy one.

- Don't over decorate the room. Keep it simple and clean. You don't want to create energy in the washroom, as it will only get flushed down the toilet.
- Install a mirror on the wall or door directly across from the toilet, reflecting it back into the room.
- Install a mirror on the outside of the washroom, either on the wall or door to reflect the store's energy back into the selling space. Don't reflect the front door. Skip the mirror if that's the only possible location.
- Keep the room well ventilated and well lit.

People don't spend much time in the store. What can I do?
When customers seem to be walking in, looking around and walking out again, you might have one of several problems.

Problem: Stale air
When we feel like the air in a store is stagnant, we leave quickly to catch a breath. Unfortunately, this is rarely a conscious thought but one that is part of our survival system.
Solutions: Add ceiling or floor fans, keep the air-conditioning on low and keep the doors open (weather permitting).
Problem: Fixtures visually blocking entrance
Solution: Move or re-angle the fixtures, angling the most visible floor fixtures to allow for the optimum amount of viewing.

3. Problem: It smells funny.
Bad odors can be caused by a variety of things: stale cigarette smoke wafting in from the "smokers' hallway," microwaved food, an unclean microwave or refrigerator, mold, someone tracked in dog doo, a child performed some biological function and the parent left without

cleaning it up, mingled odors from the gyro place on your left and the manicure parlor on your right, and so on. Some people are very scent sensitive and can't shop in stores that use air fresheners, chemical cleaners or floral aromas. Yankee Candle alternately attracts and repels customers depending on the candle scent they are featuring weekly.

Solutions: *Stale cigarette smoke, food odors and wafting odors from other stores* can be softened with air purifiers, fans in the unseen areas, or mesh bags filled with "odor-eating" pellets.

Biological odors may be removed with Natures Miracle (typically used for pets, but works for humans as well).

Chemical cleaners may be replaced in many cases with a mix of vinegar and water.

Mold must be removed at the source. Not only does it smell, but also it is terrible for your health.

Aroma nontherapy is usually due to strong floral scents. Try food-based scents such as apple, cinnamon, peach, oranges and grapefruit scents.

4. Problem: An unfriendly sales associate

This person can make or break a smaller store. The person's energy can permeate the space. People who feel uncomfortable or criticized by a salesperson rarely buy and if they do, it's often their last purchase. Unless you are giving the merchandise away, people won't put up with feeling bad in a store.

Solution: You might have to move that person into another, less visible position in the store or let him go. Very often this type of person can be intimidating. Please remember that it's either him or your business.

An upscale store opened in Westport, Connecticut. It was owned and managed by a young, married couple.

They put a fortune into the custom fixtures, displays and great merchandise. Then the husband's mother came to work at the store and was seated in a raised chair on the raised floor behind the wrap desk. She seemed to tower over customers, and her critical attitude to those she didn't like eventually slowed down sales to the point of having to close the store. Imagine trying to fire your mother! It's best to not get yourself in that spot in the first place.

I have a step up to another floor level and I worry about people falling, as well as ADA issues. What should I do?

A floor-level change is difficult in any type of store. Unless it's well marked, customers can trip over one step. For those on crutches or in wheelchairs, it becomes a small nightmare.

Solution: Block off a good portion of the raised area with fixtures pushed up to the step along the perimeter. Create a ramp at least 4 feet wide where you want your main access to the higher floor. On either side of the ramp, position cubes or tables to keep people from falling off the sides. In this way, you have a safe floor-level change that is accessible for all people.

There are lots of angles in the structure of the building. Is this bad Feng Shui?

Angles can cause arguments and dissension. Energy also gets trapped in the points of sharp angles.

Solutions: Add plants under the angled areas to soften and disperse the energy. Crystals will accomplish the same task. Lights will keep the energy from stagnating in an angled area. Also, avoid storing "stuff" in an angled area unless it is well covered with a floor-to-ceiling door and is stocked neatly within.

Are leaky roofs just annoying or are they bad luck?
A leaky roof is considered to be very unlucky. It can affect the overall energy of your store and sales.

Solution: Work with your landlord to get it fixed as quickly as possible. There are always "good" reasons why some retailers can't get the roof fixed right away. The only thing that matters is that it's done quickly. Any leaks – in plumbing, windows, and roofs or under doors – undermine the integrity of your store.

Replace stained ceiling tiles immediately. Don't wait for the roof to be fixed if it looks like it might take awhile. Your customers don't know about your problems with your landlord – and they don't care. A stained roof reflects poorly on your merchandise.

What should I do if I have no stockroom space?
If your store genuinely has no stockroom, there are several resolutions to the problem. If, however, there is one but it's too small, there are several other solutions.

Solutions: If there is no stockroom and you have some space outside in the back of the store, you can rent or buy a trailer and shelve it like a stockroom to use it for your storage.

Another solution is to build fixtures that have storage in their bases. Your wall system can be built up from the floor to include shelved storage (with doors) at 2 feet from the floor.

Do not create storage above your walled merchandise. Unless it is totally blocked from view by doors and displays, overhead storage is visually distracting, energetically overwhelming and terrible Feng Shui. The only way it can work is if the storage area is invisible to your customers and is neat and clean once the doors are opened.

Whatever you choose to do in a small stockroom, first shelve to the ceiling and then throw out anything you don't absolutely need.

What do I do about the exposed beam directly over the cash register where I stand every day?
Overhead beams feel uncomfortable over time as they compress energy as well as feel heavy and dangerous.

Solutions: First, try to move your register or the desk. Second, add some desk lamps that shoot light on the beam to "lighten" the energy. Third, soften the beam with fabric draped artistically over it so it blends better with the ceiling. This solution requires a good eye and the perfect fabric that works with both your ceiling and décor.

Almost every problem has a solution. Your intuition and intent will guide you to find the perfect way to correct an area that doesn't seem to work in your store.

The end of this book is the beginning for you, the reader.

Five Feng Shui Rules to Remember

1. Find the Balance of Yin and Yang in all you do.

2. Create the Balance of the five Elements in your surroundings.

3. Put all Actions into effect with Conscious Intent.

4. Allow Energy to flow freely throughout your space.

5. Everything you do must be positive for all concerned.

You now have many different Feng Shui and practical visual merchandising tools to bring better luck, prosperity and energy to your store. Remember the keyword before you apply any change is **intention**.

Think before you place or move anything. Know what you want to achieve. Once you recognize and understand the needs of your customers, yourself, your staff and the store, you can implement changes with grace and wisdom.

The last word to remember and cherish is **thankfulness**. Count the good things in your life every day rather than dwelling on the bad. For everything negative, there is a positive. Remember the Yin and Yang symbol. There is a balance of light and dark in everything. Know that when life seems the darkest, there is always a balancing light in our lives. Be thankful for that balance, for it is a great gift to us in this world.

Referrals, References and Sources

Each of the experts listed in this section has been an essential contributor to my education and research for this book and is often quoted or referenced throughout the chapters. All of the experts consult and are happy to work with retailers. Several of the books authored by these contributors were used for references or quotes in this book.

When searching for a Feng Shui consultant, it makes sense to work with someone who is located fairly close to your store. The experts that also have schools can refer "geographically desirable" graduates from their excellent programs.

Although I have studied Feng Shui since the early 90s, I have learned a great deal more while doing research for this book. If you discover that you've enjoyed this book and want to add to your knowledge, the authors listed below (in alphabetical order) have a lot more to offer.

Richard Craze is a Feng Shui practitioner who consults for both homeowners and businesses on creating harmonious environments. He lives in Devon, England.

His books include: *Instant Feng Shui: The Chinese Art of Living in Harmony with Your Surroundings,* Barnes & Noble Books, 2002; and *Feng Shui for Beginners,* Headway Books, 1999.

Master Lam Kam Chuen is a medical practitioner, a master of Tai Chi and Chi Kung, and a master in both Buddhist and Taoist Feng Shui. Chuen is the first Chinese Feng Shui expert to author a book on this subject for a Western audience.

His books include: **Feng Shui Handbook: How to Create a Healthier Living and Working Environment**, Henry Holt and Company, 1996; *The Way of Energy,* Gaia Books, 1991; and *Step-by-Step Tai Chi,* Gaia Books Ltd., 1994.

Contact information:
Sifu Lam Kam Chuen
1 Hercules Road
London SE1 7DP
United Kingdom
Phone: +44-7831-802-598
Fax: +44-020-7261-9049

Terah Kathryn Collins is a founder of The Western School of Feng Shui, a nationally known residential and commercial consultant, speaker and teacher of Feng Shui.

Her books, all published by Hay House Inc., include: *The Western Guide to Feng Shui: Creating Balance, Harmony, and Prosperity in Your Environment,* 1996; *The Western Guide to Feng Shui: Room by Room,* 1999; *Home Design with Feng Shui A-Z,* 2001; and the audio cassettes/workbook *Introduction to Feng Shui: The Western Guide to Feng Shui,* 1997.

Contact information:
The Western School of Feng Shui
P.O. Box 946
Solana Beach, CA 92075-0946
Phone: 800-300-6785
Fax: 760-633-1608
Email: information@wsfs.com
www.wsfs.com

Stephen Devine has an extensive background in Feng Shui consulting and teaching. He has designed and presented Feng Shui workshops internationally for more than two decades. In 1994, Devine founded The International School of Feng Shui located in Amsterdam. He developed the curriculum for the first Feng Shui Professional Training Program, which he has taught in the United States, Europe and Asia. In his teaching, he has combined his broad experience as a Feng Shui consultant with his knowledge of Ka-so (Japanese Feng Shui), Directionalology (Energy of Direction), Oriental Astrology (Nine Star Ki) and 12 Animal Astrology, enabling him to make the totality of these Eastern teachings accessible and applicable in the West.

Peggy Doscher has a Master's Certificate in Advanced Interior Alignment and uses a variety of modalities during a consultation. These may include Synchro-Alignment, Seven Star Blessing Space Clearing, advice on clutter clearing, traditional feng shui adjustments and cures, Flower Essences, Essential Oils, Sound, Sacred Symbols and Sprays. She usually works with her clients over a period of time to allow for integration periods after each visit. In this way she and her client can work through the layers at a pace that suits each clients lifestyle and commitment. Her desire is to empower her clients to tap in to their own inner resources and to facilitate this process. Peggy has created a line of pure Space Clearing Sprays that work for specific issues in a space. Each has it's own powerful energy and unique, lovely scent.

Contact information:
Dynamic Feng Shui
P.O.Box 1709
Ketchum, ID 83340
208 720-3350
www.dynamicfengshui.com
email: dynamicfengshui@yahoo.com

David Daniel Kennedy is an internationally recognized Feng Shui practitioner, teacher and consultant for residential and commercial properties.

He is the author of: *Feng Shui for Dummies,* Hungry Minds, Inc., 2001; and *Feng Shui Tips for a Better Life,* Storey Publishing, 1998.

Contact information:
International Institute for Grandmaster Lin Yun Studies
PMB 127

1563 Solano Avenue
Berkeley, CA 94707
Phone: 888-470-2727
Fax: 510-237-7374
Email: dkennedy@earthlink.net
www.fengshuiweb.com

Master Peter Leung is the creator of Feng Shui S.O.S. – Simple, Original Solutions. He consults, trains, lectures and gives workshops throughout the United States and Canada. Leung's simple personal philosophy is to try to live our lives with the compassion of the Buddha in our hearts; and to use our knowledge, talents and abilities to help all those in need regardless of their circumstances. He has taught throughout Canada and the United States, as well as in Europe and India, and has earned the well-deserved reputation of being a most generous teacher. He has also served as the "resident expert" on America Online's Feng Shui Board, and is a director of the Feng Shui Association of Canada. He works and resides with his family in Toronto.

His public online discussion list can be found at: http://groups.yahoo.com/group/fourpillars-fengshui

Contact information:
Feng Shui SOS Ltd.
P.O. Box 44540
2376 Eglinton Avenue East
Toronto, ON M1K 5K3
Canada
Phone: 416-288-9238
Email: Pleung1005@aol.com
www.FengShuiSOS.com and www.sosfengshui.com

Denise Linn has researched spiritual practices from cultures throughout the world for more than 30 years. Linn originated the unique and groundbreaking Feng Shui system called Interior Alignment, and is a renowned lecturer, author and visionary.

She is the author of numerous books, including: *Sacred Space: Clearing and Enhancing the Energy of Your Home,* Wellspring Ballantine, 1995; *Past Lives, Present Dreams,* Wellspring Ballantine, 1997; *Feng Shui for the Soul,* Hay House, 2000; and *Space Clearing,* Ebury Press, 2000.

Contact information:
Denise Linn Seminars
P.O. Box 759
Paso Robles, CA 93447
Email: DreamSeed@aol.com
www.deniselinn.com

Wendye Pardue is an experienced and excellent Feng Shui practitioner and real estate agent in Fairfield County, Connecticut. Her specialty is working with Feng Shui for homes as well as commercial properties. Pardue has a deep, intuitive feeling for Feng Shui combined with years of extensive study and practice.

Contact information:
Email: wendye1@optonline.net

Sarah Rossbach wrote the first book in the United States on Feng Shui after studying extensively with Master Lin Yun. Her books started many people on the path of learning more about Feng Shui. Rossbach was and continues to be a major influence on many practitioners today.

She is the author of numerous books, including: *Feng Shui, The Chinese Art of Placement,* E.P. Dutton, 1983; *Living*

Color: Master Lin Yu's Guide to Feng Shui and the Art of Color, Kodansha America, 1994; *Interior Design with Feng Shui*, Penguin Books, 2000; and *Feng Shui Design: From History and Landscape to Modern Gardens and Interiors*, Viking Books, 1998.

Nancy SantoPietro was the former chairperson of the first Feng Shui studies department in the United States. SantoPietro is an internationally known lecturer and teacher who designs training programs for Feng Shui consultants. She has offices in Brooklyn, New York, and Seattle and consults for both homes and businesses throughout the country.

She is the author of: **Feng Shui: Harmony by Design**, Perigee Books, 1996. In addition, her mail-order business, Gone with the Wind . . . Chimes, offers a wide array of Feng Shui products and services. A mail-order catalog is available by calling or writing:

Gone with the Wind . . . Chimes
1957 86th St.
Suite #108
Brooklyn, NY 11214
Phone: 718-256-8773

Contact information:
Nancy SantoPietro & Associates
1684 80th Street
Brooklyn, NY 11214
Phone: 718-256-2640
Email: nsanpietro@aol.com

William Spear is a world-famous teacher and consultant. In addition to offering many introductory and advanced courses to the general public, Spear conducts a professional training program in intuitive Feng Shui for architects, designers and practitioners and maintains a private practice with offices in New York, London and Litchfield, Connecticut.

He is the author of: *Feng Shui Made Easy,* Harper SanFrancisco, 1995.

Contact information:
William Spear
24 Village Green Drive
Litchfield, CT 06759
Phone: 860-567-8801
Fax: 860-567-3304

Sharon Stasney integrates Chinese medicine, traditional Feng Shui teachings, Jungian psychology and shadow-therapy work into her Feng Shui consultations. Stasney runs Self Start, a training center in Salt Lake City that provides advanced business training and mentoring for Feng Shui consultants, professional organizers and life coaches.

She is the author of: *Feng Shui Your Work Spaces,* Sterling Publishing, 2004; *Feng Shui Living,* Sterling/Chapelle, 2003; and *Feng Shui Your Kitchen,* Chapelle, 2002.

Contact information:
Self Start, Inc.
703 E. 1700 S.
Salt Lake City, UT 84105
Phone: 801-519-9161
Email: fstc@xmission.com

The Feng Shui Training Center
P.O. Box 567
Salt Lake City, UT 84110

Phone: 877-470-7769
www.thefengshuitrainingcenter.com

Clear & Simple
Phone: 801-463-9090
Email: info@clearsimple.com
www.ClearSimple.com
Elliot Jay Tanzer, the cofounder of the Integrative School of Feng Shui, has lectured, consulted and taught nationally on Feng Shui, astrology and metaphysics.

He is the author of: *Choose the Best House for You: The Feng Shui Checklist,* 2003; *Feng Shui Master Formula Study Sheets for Students and Beginning Practitioners; Tutorial for Using the Feng Shui Master Formulas Study Guides; Exercises for the Spiritual Body* – Book and Meditation Tape; *Feng Shui: For Success, Harmony & Health – A Complete Home Study Course*

All books and study materials available through at www.ElliotTanzer.com.

Contact information:
Email: info@ElliotTanzer.com
Phone: 310-281-6798

Lillian Too is one of the worlds' foremost authorities and authors on Feng Shui. Too lives in Kuala Lumpur where she consults, writes and runs her own publishing company. She is a graduate of the Harvard Business School and was the managing director of banking and retail giants in Hong Kong during the 80s before starting her prolific writing, teaching and consulting career.

She is the author of numerous books, including: *The Illustrated Encyclopedia of Feng Shui,* Element Books/Barnes &

Noble Books, 2000; *Lillian Too's Irresistible Feng Shui Magic,* Element Books, 2001; *Lillian Too's Basic Feng Shui,* North American Edition, Oriental Publications/Konsep Books, 1997; *Feng Shui Essentials,* Rider, 1997; *Lillian Too's Easy-to-Use Feng Shui: 168 Ways to Success,* Sterling Publishing, 1999; *Feng Shui,* Konsep Books, 1993; *Creating Abundance with Feng Shui,* Rider, 1999; *Feng Shui Good Fortune Symbols,* Konsep Books, 1999; and *Lillian Too's Feng Shui Kit,* Element Books, 1997.

Contact information:
www.lillian-too.com
www.wofs.com

Derek Walters is a world-renowned author of books on Chinese astrology and geomancy, including: *The Feng Shui Handbook: A Practical Guide to Chinese Geomancy and Environmental Harmony,* The Aquarian Press, 1991.

Contact information:
Hands Farm
Middlefield Lane
Newbold-on-Stour
Warwickshire CV37 8TX
United Kingdom
Phone: +44 (0)1789 459 288
Fax: +44 (0)1789 459 287
www.fengshui-school.co.uk/foundation.htm

Nancilee Wydra, cofounder of the Feng Shui Institute of America, teaches nationwide and produces an international Feng Shui newsletter, Windwater.

She is a prolific and highly regarded author of several books, including: *Feng Shui: The Book of Cures,* McGraw-Hill, 1996; *Look Before You Love: Feng Shui Techniques for Revealing Anyone's True Nature,* Contemporary Books, 1998; *Feng Shui Principles for Building and Remodeling: Creating a Space That Meets Your Needs and Promotes Well-Being*, McGraw-Hill, 2002; *Feng Shui and How to Look Before You Love,* McGraw-Hill, 1999; *101 Ways Feng Shui Can Change Your Life,* McGraw-Hill, 2002; and *Designing Your Happiness: A Contemporary Look at Feng Shui,* Heian International, 1995.

Contact information:
The Feng Shui Institute of America
7547 Bruns Court
Canal Winchester, OH 43110
Phone: 614-837-8370
Fax: 614-834-9760
Email: windwater@windwater.com
www.windwater.com

Glossary

A

Abundance:
This is a term not just for a very great quantity of wealth but also of health, success, joy and all good things. While there might be an abundance of sadness or ill-tempered customers, abundance is not used in that context in this book.

Asymmetrical:
This term can mean irregular, lopsided, uneven or unbalanced. In the context of this book, it means an arrangement or display that is not balanced in a formal way. For example: Formal balance = two paintings side by side with three related books lined up below each painting. Informal or asymmetrical balance = one large painting, one smaller painting and a third even smaller painting side by side creating an angle that leads to five books spread out flat in a fan-like shape.

B

Bagua:
This is one of the foundations of Feng Shui. It is the sacred octagon that is derived from the I Ching, one of the world's oldest and most profound methods of reading energy patterns. The Bagua is a tool for understanding the energy patterns of your store, home and office. Bagua in Chinese means "eight sign." The Bagua system helps you discover which parts of your store affect which areas of your life. There are nine sections of the Bagua (eight sides plus the center).

Below are the Bagua sections and their store areas with the corresponding colors for each area:

Bagua Section	Store Area	Color
Helpful people	front right corner	gray
Career	front center	black
Knowledge	front left	blue
Family	middle left side	green/ blue
Wealth	back, left corner	purple
Fame	back center	red
Marriage	back right corner	pink
Children	middle, right side	white
Health and Unity	center	yellow

Based on the Black Sect Tantric Buddhist School of Feng Shui, sections are in relation to the front wall of the store floor plan. The front wall is the one that contains the front door.

With thanks to David Daniel Kennedy, *Feng Shui Tips for a Better Life*, Storey Books, 1998.

Bagua Mirror:
This octagonal mirror is used to deflect poison arrows. The traditional Bagua mirror is usually painted with a red background on the frame to amass Yang (masculine) energy. Traditional Chinese trigrams are placed around the mirror in their respective areas. The center round mirror reflects and returns all the hostile energy coming from the direction of the poison arrow. A mirror cut into an octagonal shape will also work. Paint the back of it red to increase its negativity-reflecting power.

Balance:
This means being in a state of equilibrium, symmetry and stability. Balance in design means an equal emphasis on all areas of the design: equality in weight or amount. In Feng Shui, balance is achieved when the two complementary yet opposing forces of Yin and Yang are in harmony. There are equal amounts of Yin (female) and Yang (male) energies in a space.

Black Sect Tantric Buddhist Feng Shui (BSTBFS):
This eclectic school of Feng Shui is a working philosophy that postulates that the best results come from a marriage of Eastern and Western viewpoints and knowledge. It weaves together a combination of traditional

Feng Shui, the teachings of India, China and Tibet along with Grandmaster Lin Yun's energy theories. Grandmaster Lin Yun brought together many different studies to create BSTBFS.

Traditional Feng Shui schools employ a physical compass to diagnose the key directions of the space and relate them to the occupants through astrological calculations. BSTBFS acknowledges the validity of the traditional Compass method but uses a different approach. It employs a "mental" compass, the Bagua, to read the energies of the space based on the entryway.

The importance of intention as a sixth sense in addition to the five known senses – sight, hearing, touch, taste and smell – also differentiates BSTBFS from the traditional schools.

With thanks to David Daniel Kennedy, *Feng Shui for Dummies*, Hungry Mind, 2001.

C

Chi:
This is a highly powerful invisible force, yet we can feel energy when we "tune in" to a space. Chi flows like wind or water, like a river of energy. The main source of this energy river in your body is your mouth. In your store or home, it's your front door.

Beneficial Characteristics: Negative Characteristics of Chi Flow of Ideal Chi Flow:

- Powerful—rushing energy (moving too fast, unbalancing)
- Positive—stagnant chi (prevents goals from being achieved)
- Uplifting—blocked chi (can stop your progress in life)
- Flowing—leaking chi (leads to a loss of energy)
- Smooth—piercing chi (may threaten your health and welfare)

With thanks to David Daniel Kennedy, *Feng Shui for Dummies*.

"All matter has vibration. Referred to as chi by the Chinese, ki by the Japanese and prana or Brahmin by the people of India, this invisible electromagnetic energy radiates in particular patterns from objects of all shapes and sizes."

With thanks to William Spear, *Feng Shui Made Easy*, HarperSanFrancisco, 1995.

Compass School of Feng Shui: This ancient and highly respected school uses the compass directions to create good Feng Shui. The formulas, based on directional orientation, are based on the dates of birth and the sex of the inhabitants of the space. This method believes that directions and timing are two of the most critical factors that determine the Feng Shui of a space. Also known as the Eight Mansions Formula, this school of Feng Shui customizes auspicious and inauspicious directions, locations and colors to attract:
- Success
- Wealth
- Love
- Marriage
- Health
- Career growth
- Personal development
- Academic success

Creative Cycle:
The five elements generate, create or lead to one another in a continuous chain of creative energy. Each element changes from one form to another.
1. Wood, as it burns, is the fuel for Fire.
2. Ashes, the result of Fire, return to and replenish the Earth.
3. The Earth gives birth to Metal.
4. Metal, heated sufficiently, becomes liquid like Water.
5. Water nourishes Wood – and the cycle continues forever.

With thanks to David Daniel Kennedy, *Feng Shui for Dummies*.

Cures:
These are methods or remedies to change the negative energy created by chi that is not flowing in harmony with the environment.

D

Dead Zone:
The area in your store where merchandise goes to die.

Destructive cycle:
The five elements symbolically destroy each other in a continuous pattern.
1. Wood is cut by the ax (Metal).
2. Metal is burned by the blacksmith's Fire.
3. Fire is extinguished by Water.
4. Water is absorbed and subdued by the Earth.
5. Earth is penetrated by growing trees (Wood).

With thanks to David Daniel Kennedy, *Feng Shui for Dummies.*

E

Earth:
This is the element that most represents Feng Shui at work. Feng Shui is the luck of the earth and is an important component in the correct practice of Feng Shui. The center of the store, home or office is represented by the earth element. The energy of the earth element is stability. Its corresponding color is yellow; materials are clay, brick, mud and cement; and shapes are squares, rectangles and cubes.

Eight Mansions School of Feng Shui:
This is the ancient school of Feng Shui that works with astrology and is combined with the Compass School.

Elements:
The five elements and their interactions make up the theory of Wuxing – the Chinese name for the five elements. The balance of elements in a space helps determine the quality of the chi energy and the fang shun. Understanding the Creative and Destructive cycles for the elements and the natural location of the elements in your store will aid in "curing" any problems you might have.

Energy:
Also know as Chi or Qui. Energy is found in all things – alive or man-made. Energy can flow or be blocked or stagnate. The flow of energy is what creates good or bad Feng Shui.

Enhancers, Enhancements:
Good fortune symbols that, if correctly placed, create good Feng Shui. There are many different symbols of good fortune that can be used to enhance the Feng Shui of corners and rooms. An excellent resource book for this is *The Illustrated Encyclopedia of Feng Shui* by Lillian Too, Barnes & Noble Books, 1999.

Entity:
A thing with a distinct existence, an object, phenomenon, element, unit or organism. It can also mean life, being, existence, essence and quintessence.

F

Façade:
The publicly acknowledged front or face of a building.

Feng Shui:
Feng Shui, which translates to wind and water in Chinese, is the marriage of the practical and the metaphysical. One of the oldest known disciplines in the world, Feng Shui is the science and art of arranging a living or working space to allow for the positive flow of beneficial energy or chi combined with the balance of elements to create good health, luck, happiness and wealth.

Fire:
This is one of the five basic elements. Fire is represented by all forms of lighting, as well as natural sunlight, anything to do with animals, art that shows people or animals, sunshine, light or fire, triangles, cones or pyramids and the red spectrum of colors. The energy of fire is active. The fire element activates leadership qualities and encourages healthy emotional interactions between people. Too much fire in an environment stimulates aggression, impatience and impulsive behavior. Too little fire can create emotional coldness.

With thanks to Terah Kathryn Collins, *The Western Guide to Feng Shui,* Hay House, 1996, and *The Western Guide to Feng Shui: Room by Room,* Hay House, 1999.

Flying Star Feng Shui:
Flying Star Feng Shui is the traditional style of Feng Shui that the Asian peoples have practiced for centuries. Flying Star Feng Shui

determines favorable and unfavorable time periods and locations in an environment, as well as monthly, annual and 20-year cycles. It also pinpoints specific locations to energize for stronger relationships and greater prosperity. Flying Star Feng Shui is the analysis of chi and the subsequent patterns generated in accordance with the geomagnetic directional patterns that affect the structures in which we live and work.

As with so many aspects of ancient Chinese practices, Flying Star Feng Shui is strongly based on the I Ching. Flying Star Feng Shui uses these methods of I Ching-based interactive analysis to instruct us as to the condition of our homes and businesses, and how to remedy problems caused by structures, or items within the structures, that fall out of harmony with the sea of energy patterns within which they (and we) reside.

With thanks to Scott Ransom, Portland, Oregon.

Form School:
One of the oldest types of Feng Shui, Form School evaluates the chi and balance of Yin and Yang in the surrounding mountains, hills, roads, structures and waterways to determine good or bad Feng Shui.

With thanks to www.fengshuiboston.com.

Formula Feng Shui:
This is a very exacting school of Feng Shui that uses mathematical formulas to determine the best placement of buildings, rooms, objects and furniture. Water Formula Feng Shui is part of the Formula School and employs precise formulas to attract wealth and prosperity using water features. Dimensions Formula Feng Shui uses a Feng Shui ruler to calculate the best dimensions for homes, rooms and furniture.

G

Gazing Ball:
A mirrored sphere about 12 to 14 inches in diameter can be used to deflect poison arrows both indoors and out.

Good Luck:
Luck is an abstract term and in Feng Shui it refers to the accomplishment or possession of specific categories of good fortune. Feng Shui lists eight types of good luck – wealth, health, family and relationships, children, having a good name, having a good career, having a good education and having the goodwill of powerful people. Chinese divination readings define luck as different types of grades of luck for each of these eight categories. Money and wealth luck is subdivided into the luck of inheritance, the luck of gambling and speculation, and the luck of business success. In the language of Feng Shui, luck has many different meanings.

With thanks to Lillian Too, author of *The Illustrated Encyclopedia of Feng Shui.*

H

Harmony:
A pleasing arrangement or combination of parts to create an aesthetic effect. In Feng Shui, it is the harmonious interaction of the elements of earth, fire, water, metal and wood. For true harmony to exist, the elements must enhance one another.

I

I-Ching:
Also known as The Book of Changes, this is the major source book of Feng Shui and probably the main source book of most of China's cultural practices. All that is great and significant in Chinese cultural history takes inspiration from the I-Ching. Both branches of Chinese philosophy – Confucianism and Taoism – have their common roots in this ancient classic. The origins of the I-Ching go back to mythical times as a book of divination and wisdom. It introduced the many related principles and symbols of the Chinese predictive sciences. Its view of the trinity (heaven, earth and man), the concepts of Yin and Yang (balance and harmony, positive and negative forces, good fortune and misfortune) are derived from interpretations of the texts of the I-Ching.

With thanks to Lillian Too, author of *The Illustrated Encyclopedia of Feng Shui.*

Inauspicious:
This term refers to anything that is ill-omened, unlucky, ill-fated, doomed, unfortunate – generally awful.

Intent:
The resolve, aim or purpose of an individual is his or her intent.

J

Jade Plant:
Jade is an auspicious plant that is regarded as the wealth plant. In China, storeowners will place jade plants in their store windows to attract customers.

K

Karma:
This term refers to the effect on your life from past actions: what goes around comes around; as you sow, so shall you reap. As life is ongoing, past actions affect your consciousness, your life lessons and your ultimate success as a human being. Webster's dictionary describes karma as: "In Hinduism and Buddhism, the ethical consequences of the totality of one's actions that determine the destiny of one's subsequent existence or existences until one has achieved spiritual liberation" or Nirvana.

L

Lamp:
This term has at least two distinct meanings. In the lighting industry, lamp is another word for light bulb. In common terms, it applies to a light fixture complete with a bulb, a plug, a base and a shade that is either decorative or purely functional.

With thanks to Judith Bell, author of *Silent Selling*, Fairchild Publications, 2002.

In Feng Shui, lamps are used to stimulate Yang energy and are usually excellent placed anywhere. They fuel good energy. Muted, warm lights are always better than harsh white lights.

With thanks to Lillian Too, *The Illustrated Encyclopedia of Feng Shui.*

Landscape Feng Shui:
The school and study of Feng Shui that works with the plot of land your building is on and the surrounding areas is Landscape Feng Shui.

"Garden or landscape Feng Shui is a method of extending and balancing the harmonies established inside the home or business with forms and shapes, light and shade, perhaps incorporating water and other features, to influence the flow of positive chi. Indoor and outdoor Feng Shui must work in harmony to encourage the flow of beneficial chi from the landscaped environment into your living or work space."

With thanks to www.fengshuiboston.com.

Lo Pan:
This is the authentic Chinese geomancer's compass – a highly complex instrument comprised of up to 36 concentric rings drawn around a small magnetic compass. For the layman, the use of the Lo Pan can be confusing unless accompanied by extensive study leading to great knowledge. It is much easier to use a Western style compass when working with directional Feng Shui.

Lucky Numbers:
Numerology combined with Chinese theories can make your life very confusing. The Chinese find certain numbers unlucky because they sound like negative words in Chinese. For example, four is considered to be the death number because phonetically it sounds like "sey" or "die" in Chinese. In Western numerology, four can be very lucky but is associated with hard work helping to create that luck. In Chinese, the combination of two and three is considered extremely inauspicious as it leads to misunderstandings, quarrels and other problems. Two and three add up to five, which is the number in the Chinese system that brings nothing but problems and difficulties. In Western thought, five can mean constant change, or expect the unexpected. Either way, five is only for the adventurous spirit. Only you know what your lucky number is

because it's brought you luck at different times in your life.

M

Manifesting:
The process we use to make something happen. Manifest means to show plainly to the eye or mind; to display or show by one's acts; to materialize. Manifesting is a term used to describe the positive methods one takes to create a more positive situation, life or reality.

Metal:
The metal element enhances mental clarity and independence and strengthens presence of mind, even during stressful times. Too much metal creates mental and emotional rigidity, stubbornness, lack of teamwork and the inability to compromise. Too little metal promotes indecisiveness, procrastination and confusion. The metal element is found in all metals, cement, rocks and stones, natural crystals and gemstones, art and sculpture made from metal or stone, circular, oval and arched shapes, and white and light pastel colors.

With thanks to Terah Kathryn Collins, author of *The Western Guide to Feng Shui: Room by Room.*

N

Nine, Multiples of:
Feng Shui teaches that nine is the highest number and it symbolizes completion and power. Using its multiples in your Feng Shui cures can add potency to any remedy.

With thanks to David Daniel Kennedy, author of *Feng Shui for Dummies.*

O

Open Shelves:
These can resemble knives and can create poison arrows. Their sharp edges send out Shar chi, killing breath, and with it illness, loss of income and even a dramatic reduction in wealth. In retail, however, shelves are a necessity. One cure is to place the merchandise flush with the edge of the shelf to soften its sharp edge. Make sure all glass shelves have polished edges and if possible, curve their ends to avoid real accidents. When you use dimensional (thick) shelves, you alleviate some of these problems.

P

Parabolic:
This is a type of reflecting metal insert that goes into fluorescent light fixtures that focuses the light onto the selling floor rather than allowing it to "bounce back" onto the ceiling.

Pathways:
Winding pathways and/or aisles are always considered to be better Feng Shui than straight paths. Energy accumulates and strengthens in a positive way when it meanders through a store rather than rushing from end to end.

Pegboard:
This is a wall system that comes in 4-by-8-foot sheets of masonite with a grid of small holes. Usually seen in hardware stores from the 1940's and 50's, it is making a comeback with different surface materials.

Pillars or Columns:
These are only a problem if they face the front door directly. Square pillars can cause more harm than round ones. Mirroring the column on three sides (not the side reflecting the front door) is one solution, but the best solution is to place a large, round-leafed plant at the corner of the offending column edge.

Pod:
A retail pod is a grouping of like items on the selling floor. For example, a pod at a hardware store might include all the tools and accessories needed to build a bookcase. The display could be a small handmade bookcase on a riser (platform) holding and surrounded by the tools and materials used in its construction. In a bridal shop, a pod might consist of a mannequin or form wearing a wedding dress next to a table showing all the possible accessories, plus flowers that work with the dress.

With thanks to Ken Mantel for giving me the word, "pod."

Poison Arrows:
These are created by structures in the environment that send negative energy toward you, your store, your home or your office. A poison arrow is any sharp angle, point or protruding corner aimed at your environment. These sharp points can be anything from a neighbor's protruding roof ridge, a tree branch or corner of a building to the sharp edges of a sculpture, furniture or wall corner. The most dangerous poison arrows are those that point toward your front door.

Q

Qui:
This is another spelling for chi, or energy.

R

Rectangular Shapes:
These represent the wood element and are considered to be very lucky. The essence of the wood element is that it symbolizes growth, so rectangular shapes are seen as enhancers of growth.

Red Thread:
Red thread or ribbon is always used to tie together Chinese coins. Red is a Yang color and infuses good-luck objects with alive, animated energy.

Remedy:
Remedy is another word for cure.

S

Shamanism:
The spiritual practice of ancient civilizations and cultures, Shamanism is the oldest healing tradition in the world. The Shaman in history served as the communicator between the physical and spiritual worlds through various rituals and visualizations. This tradition is observed by modern mankind as a way of returning to its roots.

With thanks to http://healing.about.com.

Smoking a Space:
To clear negative energy out of a space, you can do what Native Americans have done for centuries – smoke it out. According to Denise Linn, in the definitive book on clearing space – Sacred Space, Ballantine Books, 1995 – this is an ancient purification ceremony.

"Spirit Smoke"
Smoke connects us to the Spirit of the Air and, throughout the ages, smoke has been used as a part of religious purification rituals in many cultures around the world. Ascending smoke forms a channel connecting us to a Great Spirit. Our prayers rise on smoke to God, and the answers to these prayers travel back to us by the same path.

Outside a Buddhist temple, there is usually an urn holding burning sticks of incense. Worshippers will stop for a moment to breathe in the smoke, or draw it to their body with cupped hands to purify themselves before entering the temple.

Smudging
A Native American traditional way of using smoke to purify a space is through the practice of smudging. Smudging is a ritual burning of herbs, using the smoke produced to alter energy for one's self or another, or to cleanse the energy of a specific space.

Sage
Sage is used as part of many Native American ceremonies because of its purification powers. In the Sun Dance Ceremony, the dancers wear wreaths of sage on their heads and chew the leaves to alleviate their thirst. Sage is associated with purity, with things of the spirit and of the heavens.

Sweetgrass
This herb is used almost universally among Native American tribal peoples. Its fresh, clean smell, which can be compared to new-mown hay, is said to drive away negative thoughts and ill spirits."

With thanks to Denise Linn, *Sacred Space.*

Cedar
Cedar can also be used for the spiritual cleansing of a space.

Spirit Guides:
All human beings have spirit guides that help us in our lives. Very often we have a team of guides at any one time. They can be beings that were once in human form or those who have always lived on the other side. Spirit guides can come and go as needed. While we might have a spirit guide that has been with us our entire life, that guide might also be looking over many other people. The sense of time and space is very different on the other side and we cannot begin to understand it in our linear-dominated Earth lives.

Very often people want to know the names of their spirit guides. Ask them. It's very likely that the first name that comes to mind is the name of the guide most present at that time. You can talk to your spirit guides and they will hear you. You can ask for help and they will try to offer advice. Whether you hear them or not is up to you.

Some people try automatic writing to better hear their guides. To try this, go into a quiet room, turn off all phones and music, and either pick up a pen or sit down at the computer.

Make an effort to empty your mind of rushing thoughts. If you know how to meditate, this is a good time to put those techniques to use to quiet down your mind. If not, visualize a vast, dark board in your mind and see what gets written on it in your imagination. Considering that your imagination is unlimited, the words and images that come up will have some immediate meaning. You can ask a question out loud or in your mind and immediately write down (without analyzing it first) whatever you "hear" in your mind or "see" on the board.

T

Ten Emperor Coins:
These are Chinese coins taken from each of the 10 emperors' reigns and tied together with red thread or cord. The coins may either be genuine antique coins from the 10 different periods or reproductions. It doesn't matter if they are real or copies – it's the intention behind using them that counts. They should be placed either behind your office chair or on the left side of your desk.

Toilets:
These are always considered to be negative Feng Shui. Keep the seat down and the door closed at all times. Don't over decorate or add expensive furnishings to the toilet area. Keep it simple and clean. Overdoing it only magnifies the bad luck.

Trees:
Trees have very positive energy for stores, homes and offices. Plant the following trees to enhance their special qualities in your life.

Tree Types	**Positive Effects**
Persimmons	joy, luck in business, good start for new endeavor
Orange	good luck
Pine	resilience, integrity, dignity, longevity
Willow (only in front)	gracefulness, scholarly atmosphere
Banana Palm	scholarly ambitions
Apple	safety
Pomegranate	fertility
Pear	sweetness
Olive	peace
Peach-plum	compassion

Excerpted from *Feng Shui for Dummies.*

U

Utility Rooms:
A utility room, stockroom or any other room that isn't part of the customers' perception of your store is still considered to be part of the

Bagua grid. These rooms must be clean, neat, well lit and free from clutter.

V

Ventilation:
Air or wind could be the sixth element for Feng Shui. It is vital that your store be well ventilated with as much fresh air coming in as possible.

W

Wall Breaks:
A wall break is an architectural element that is attached vertically from floor to ceiling to break up an expanse of wall into sections. Wall breaks are often perpendicular thin walls that come out less than 3 feet from the back wall. They can be temporary and made of Sintra board, Gatorfoam, plywood or any other rigid material with finished edges. Wall breaks can also be created by separating merchandise visually, leaving a minimum of 6 inches between groups or classifications.

Wealth Vase:
This is a vase that contains symbols of wealth and written affirmations or desires for what you want wealth to bring to you, your family and your employees. The wealth vase is traditionally hidden from view and made of earth or metal elements. The earth elements that will bring the most luck would be fine porcelain or crystal. The lucky metal elements may be silver, pewter or gold. While brass or copper will work, the better the material, the better the luck.

Wind Dancers:
These are usually mobiles, whirligigs or free-flowing banners that add energy to a space and slow down negative rushing energy.

Wood:
Wood has intrinsic life force energy. This element represents growth and is excellent to have in all four corners of your store. Energetically, the wood element aids in your intuition, creativity, flexibility and expansion. Too much wood can promote a sense of being overwhelmed, while too little can stagnate growth and inhibit creative flow and ideas.

The wood element is found in all wooden furniture, walls and accessories, plants and flowers including silk, plastic and dried, plant-based cloth such as cotton and rayon, floral fabrics, wall and floor coverings, art portraying landscapes, gardens, plants and flowers, paper, columnar shapes such as pillars, pedestals and poles, stripes, and the colors blue and green – all tones.

With thanks to Terah Kathryn Collins, *The Western Guide to Feng Shui: Room by Room.*

Y

Yang:
The essential nature of life energy, brightness, daylight and the sun, Yang is basically the life half of the Yin-Yang concept. Yang energy is symbolized by activity, by bright light and by daytime hours. Yang energy is vital for the presence of good Feng Shui in the houses of the living, but it should never be present in such excessive quantities that Yin becomes obliterated completely. When Yin is completely absent, Yang ceases to exist.

Yin:
This is considered to be death energy encompassing silence, darkness, the moon and night. Yin energy is the complete opposite of Yang energies. They never conflict but instead complement one another. They give life to each other and neither would exist without the other. Yin is darkness and silence and is excellent energy for a bedroom or other places of rest.

Yin	**Yang**
Dark colors	Light colors
Muted colors	Bright colors
Curved lines (fixtures/furniture)	Straight lines (fixtures/furniture)
Dim lighting	Bright lighting
Moist	Dry
Low (fixtures/furniture)	High
Quiet	Loud
Soft surface materials	Hard surface materials
Empty walls	Filled book shelves and wall fixtures
Decreases (dimmers)	Grows (plants)
Hides (closets, recessed lights)	Obvious (in plain view – fixtures)
Cool (windows and fans)	Warm (heating vents)
Still (chairs)	Active (fans, desk chairs with casters)
Odors (mold, smoke)	Fragrances (candles, good food)

With thanks to Nancilee Wydra, *The Book of Cures*, Contemporary Books, 1996.

Yin-Yang Symbol:

This symbol perfectly describes the concept of Yin and Yang. They are opposing yet complementary. They rely on each other to make a whole. There is a bit of Yin in the Yang – and some Yang in the Yin. It exemplifies the perfect flow of universal energy.

Index